PEOPLE IN THE

PHYSICAL
LANDSCAPE

NEIL PUNNETT

Head of Humanities

Wilberforce College Hull

Consultant editors

Richard Kemp   County Adviser for Humanities Buckinghamshire

David Maclean   Principal Adviser Essex

Formerly County Inspector for Geography

SIMON & SCHUSTER

LONDON • SYDNEY • NEW YORK • TOKYO • TORONTO

First published in Great Britain in 1987
by Macdonald & Co (Publishers) Ltd

Reprinted 1989 (twice)

Second and subsequent impressions published in
Great Britain by
Simon & Schuster Ltd
Wolsey House, Wolsey Road
Hemel Hempstead HP2 4SS

Typesetting by
Swanston Graphics Ltd
Derby

Printed in Great Britain by
BPCC Paulton Books Ltd

. **British Library Cataloguing in Publication Data**

Punnett, Neil
    People in the physical landscape.—
    (Geography for GCSE)
    1. Physical geography—Text-books—1945—
    I. Title II. Kemp, Richard III. Maclean,
    David, *1948*– III. Series
    910'.02   GB55
    ISBN 0-7501-0041-9

Series editor John Day
Editor Elizabeth Clarke
Design and art direction Liz Black
Picture research Elizabeth Loving
Production Ken Holt

Acknowledgements
The publishers thank the following for permission to reproduce their photographs and other copyright materials. The numbers refer to pages and L, R, T, B, C indicate left, right, top, bottom and centre respectively.

Aerocamera-Barthofmeester 55; Aerofilms 4(TL), 30, 50, 65, 67, 68; BBC Hulton Picture Library 34; Colorsport 41; Dorset County Council 45(B); Dundee University 16; Patrick Eagar 20(T); Geo-Science Features 6, 7, 12(T), 78; Robert Harding Picture Library 5(T), 10, 11, 44(TR), 44(BR), 93; Inghams Travel 77; Hugh McKnight 36(T); Meteorological Office 22; Municipal Gallery of Modern Art, Dublin 5(B); Nigel Press Associates 4(BR); Ordnance Survey 27, 69; Permutit 12(B); Popperfoto 35; Neil Punnett 28, 29(T), 31, 46, 92(TR), 92(BR); Betty Rawlings 92(TL), 92(BL); Rex 19, 20(C), 20(B), 86, 88; Thames Water Authority 39(T); University Film Service, California/Geo-Science Features 83; Anthony Waltham 29(C); Anthony Waltham/Gunn 32; Water Authorities Association 18(B); West Air Photography 44(L); David and Jill Wright 74, 75; ZEFA Picture Library 4(TR), 4(BL), 5(C), 38, 62, 77

Cover illustration Brian Grimwood
Illustrators
Peter Bull 8, 9(B), 18(T), 22, 32, 33(T), 39, 40(T), 45(B), 49(B), 55, 57(B), 77, 82(T), 89, 93(B)
John Ridyard 60
Swanston Graphics Ltd all maps and other diagrams

Glossary

Terms which readers may be meeting for the first time or which have a special meaning in the context of this book are listed in the glossary on pages 94 and 95. The first time such a term appears it is printed in *italic* type (except in the case of illustrations).

CONTENTS

PERCEPTIONS OF THE LANDSCAPE

The world has an enormous variety of landscapes. Seven pictures of very different landscapes are shown on these pages. Some of the landscapes seem to have been little affected by people, others owe a great deal to the work of the human race.

1 A polder landscape, Netherlands

2 Sydney, Australia

3 The Swiss Alps

4 The Earth viewed from space

5 Terraced paddy fields, China

6 The Grand Canyon, Arizona, United States

7 Waterloo Bridge, as painted by Monet (1901)

1 a) Which of the landscapes shown here do you think has been most affected by people? How has it been affected?

   b) Which do you think has been least touched by human actions?

2 Look at all the pictures. Write a list putting them in order, based on how much you would like to visit them on holiday. Then write a few sentences to explain your reasons for listing them in that order.

3 a) Which of the landscapes do you find the most 'friendly'? Why?

   b) Which do you find the most 'hostile' landscape? Why?

4 How much would you like to live permanently in each of the landscapes pictured here?
   Write a list putting them in your choice order. Explain the reasons for choosing the way you did.

5 Look at the painting. Some of the questions that follow ask you to think about your reactions to the painting, and about what you think the artist was trying to show – so there are not necessarily any 'right' answers!

   a) What is the subject of the painting? Is it mainly about a natural landscape or about a human landscape?

   b) What time of day do you think it is in the painting? What time of year do you think it is?

   c) What signs of human activity are there in the landscape?

   d) When was the picture painted? How might the landscape shown look different today?

   e) What impression of the landscape do you think Monet was trying to convey?

   f) In what ways might Monet's painting be different from a colour photograph taken at the same time (if that had been possible)?

   g) Write a paragraph to describe your feelings about the painting.

Rocks are very important to people. We use rocks in our buildings and our roads. We grow our crops in soil formed partly from pieces of rock. We wear rocks as ornaments: diamond rings, gold earrings, silver bracelets. Statues are often carved from rocks. We sprinkle rocksalt on to our food. These are just a few of the many ways in which people have used rocks for thousands of years.

Rocks are the material which makes up the Earth's crust. They consist of natural substances called *minerals*. Most people think that rocks are hard with a definite shape, such as granite. Yet sand is also a rock. It is a powder made from finely ground pieces of rock. Clay, which is soft and easily moulded, is another type of rock. There are three main groups of rock: sedimentary, igneous and metamorphic.

SEDIMENTARY ROCKS

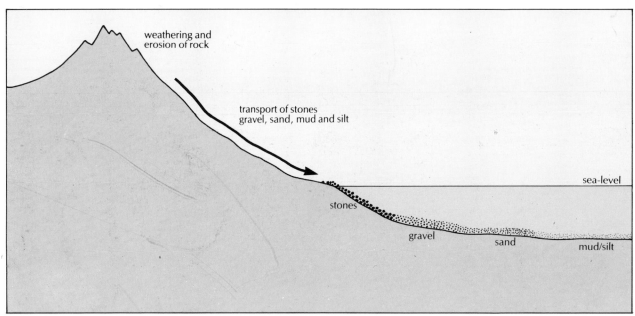

1 How the type of sedimentary rock varies with depth

These rocks are formed from material deposited on the sea-bed and river-beds or, more rarely, on land. Over a long period of time the sediment slowly builds up, layer upon layer. Pressure compacts the sediment and chemical action cements the particles together to create rock. Visual 1 shows how the type of sedimentary rock varies according to the depth of water in which it formed.

Limestone and chalk have been formed from tiny sea creatures. When they died they fell to the sea-bed where they were covered with mud. Their soft parts decayed leaving the calcium carbonate of which their shells were made. Chalk is almost pure calcium carbonate.

Coal is another rock formed from the decay of living things, in this case vegetation which grew in tropical swamps.

Many sedimentary rocks contain the fossils of animals and plants whose remains were caught in the sediment as it built up. The fossils tell us what life existed millions of years ago and can help us to date the rocks. No fossils are found in igneous rocks. Sedimentary rocks may also be distinguished from igneous rocks by the fact that they are usually deposited in layers called strata. The strata are separated from each other by bedding planes. There may also be vertical cracks in the rocks called joints.

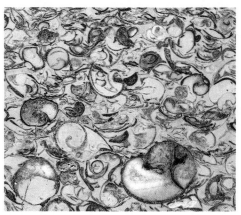

2 Limestone: a sedimentary rock

IGNEOUS ROCKS

Deep beneath the Earth's surface, the rock is so hot that it is liquid, or molten. This molten rock is called magma. Magma may be injected into the Earth's crust from beneath. As magma cools, it solidifies and forms igneous rock. Igneous rocks formed deep underground are called plutonic. They cooled slowly, so are made up of large crystals. Granite is a plutonic rock, composed of large crystals of quartz, felspar and mica. If the magma rises through the crust to the surface it is called lava. Lava will cool very quickly, so has very small crystals, as in the case of basalt. It can even have a frothy appearance, caused by escaping gases, eg pumice.

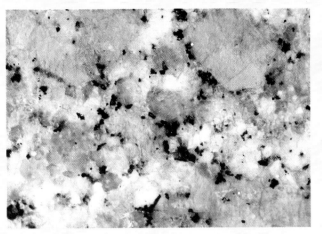

3 Granite: an igneous rock

METAMORPHIC ROCKS

These are rocks which have been changed from their original state by intense heat or pressure. Both igneous and sedimentary rock may be changed into new forms. Limestone may be changed into marble, sandstone into quartzite, clay into slate and granite into gneiss. Metamorphic rocks are usually much harder than the rocks from which they were formed.

4 Marble: a metamorphic rock

1 List ten uses of rock in everyday life.

2 What is the difference between plutonic igneous rock and lava?

3 Study the three rocks shown in Visuals 2, 3 and 4. Draw the three rocks and write notes under each drawing, explaining how the rocks were formed.

4 Copy the drawing in Visual 5 and add the following labels in the correct places:
strata   bedding plane   joint   fossil

5 What is the connection between slate and clay?

6 Using some samples of different rocks:

a) Test each rock for 'hardness' using a penknife or nail. Rank them according to how hard you think they are.

b) Write about each of the rocks including their colour, hardness and texture.

c) Try to say which of the three groups (igneous, sedimentary or metamorphic) each rock sample comes into. Give reasons for your answer.

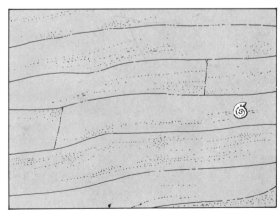

5 Fossil embedded in rock strata

3 WEATHERING

Look at the gravestone. When Theodore Jones was buried, in 1869, the gravestone bore his name clearly for all to see. It is not so easy to read now. What has happened to the stone since 1869? Over the years the action of the weather – wind, rain and frost – has eaten away the lettering and the other carvings.

There are plenty of other examples of the effects of weathering. How many can you see on your way to school?

Rocks are broken down by weathering. Weathering can be divided into three main forms: mechanical, chemical and biological.

Mechanical Weathering

This is the physical break-up of rocks. Frost is often a cause of rock fracture. Water, which finds its way into cracks and *joints* in rock, expands by 10% when it freezes. This causes great pressure. Repeated freezing and thawing weakens the rock and eventually splits it into jagged pieces. This is called frost shattering. Large amounts of these shattered rocks can be found as scree slopes in mountainous areas where frost action is, or has been, intense.

Mechanical weathering also occurs due to changes of temperature causing expansion and contraction of rock. Obviously, the greater the range of temperature, the more effective this form of weathering will be. In deserts the blistering heat of the day causes the rock's surface to expand and break away from the inner layers of rock. At night the rock's surface contracts in the cooler temperatures. As this happens daily, it will eventually cause the rock to crack. Pieces of rock drop off in layers, like the skin of an onion. This process is called exfoliation.

Chemical Weathering

Chemical weathering is caused by the action of water. Ordinary rainwater is slightly acidic and can dissolve certain minerals such as calcium carbonate in limestone. Decaying plants (and animals) produce acids which erode rocks.

Human actions have increased chemical weathering through the burning of coal, oil and gas. Sulphur dioxide gas is released by this burning process. The sulphur dioxide combines with water and oxygen in the atmosphere to form dilute sulphuric acid. *Acid rain* harms plants, animals and buildings. So, many environmental groups are now acting to get industry to reduce the amount of sulphur dioxide it discharges into the atmosphere.

1 Theodore Jones' gravestone

2 Examples of three weathering processes

weathering:
mechanical
chemical
biological

erosion:
rivers
wind
ice
sea

STORAGE

deposition:
scree
beaches
mud flats etc.

3 The weathering system

Biological Weathering

Plants and animals can cause biological weathering. The roots of trees may grow into joints and cracks in rock and force the rock apart. Burrowing animals such as moles, and even the humble earthworm, will help to break down rock.

Erosion, Transport and Deposition

Once a rock has been weakened by weathering, it is more likely to be eroded. The rock can be broken up and carried away by the agents of erosion: running water, the sea, glaciers and the wind. The agents of erosion also transport the eroded material and deposit it somewhere else. A river may undermine its bank until it collapses. The river then transports the eroded material and deposits it where the speed of water flow is reduced, such as where it enters a lake.

Weathering and the processes of erosion can be viewed as parts of a simple system, as Visual 3 shows.

1 *How can an old gravestone provide evidence that weathering has occurred?*

2 *Theodore Jones' family (Visual 1) could not afford to buy a marble gravestone, so they had to be content with a limestone one. What difference might there be in the appearance of Theodore's gravestone today if marble had been used?*

3 *Describe the type of weathering which you would expect to occur under the following conditions:*

   a) *On a mountainside in the Scottish Highlands.*

   b) *On bare rock exposed in the Great Australian Desert.*

4 *Study the three drawings in Visual 2. Copy the drawings and add labels to explain the processes of weathering which have probably affected the rocks in each case.*

5 *Why do you think a knowledge of weathering processes would help the people shown below in their jobs?*

The type of rock greatly affects the scenery of an area. A granite landscape will look very different from a landscape formed on chalk or clay, for example. Rock characteristics which influence the scenery include *hardness*, *structure* and *permeability*.

Visual 1 shows the relative hardness of major rock types. Granite will form rugged upland country with steep slopes. Clay will form flat or gently sloping lowland.

The structure of the rock includes the number and size of the individual particles of rock, the joints and bedding planes, and whether the rock has been cracked (faulted) by earth movements. Weathering will often exploit weaknesses in the rock, enlarging joints and faults and breaking up the rock.

Permeable rocks (also known as aquifers) let water drain through them. There are two types of permeable rock: porous and pervious. In porous rock water drains through holes or pores. In pervious rock water drains through cracks and joints in the rock. The water makes its way underground until it reaches the water table; below this is the saturated zone where the pores and joints are filled with water. Permeable rocks will have very few streams or rivers flowing across them.

Impermeable rocks do not let water drain through them. Landscapes of such rocks will have a lot of rivers, lakes and marshes.

Granite Landscapes

Granite forms mountainous or moorland areas. It is a non-porous rock with many streams, rivers and peat bogs. Granite is well jointed, caused by its contraction upon cooling. It is therefore somewhat pervious. Dartmoor in Devon (Visual 2) is a granite area. It rises to 612 m and is a wild, bleak moorland with few trees. The heather-clad slopes rise to blocks of bare grey rock on the summits; these are tors. Tors are probably the result of very intensive weathering under the much warmer climate which Dartmoor experienced in the past (about 25 million years ago). The less jointed granite survived longer than the more closely jointed granite and is preserved to this day in the blocks of the tors.

Granite landscapes are difficult to farm. They support poor, badly drained soils on which only sheep farming is possible and that only in more favourable areas. On the higher moors, farming has often been replaced by forestry. Granite is quarried because its hardness makes it suitable for many kinds of building. At Lee Moor on the edge of Dartmoor are china clay quarries. China clay, or kaolin, is formed

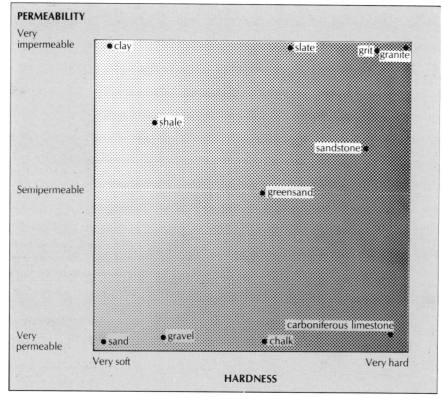

1 The hardness and permeability of rock types

2 Holwell Tor, Dartmoor: a granite landscape

by the decomposition of granite. This occurs within the Earth's crust where hot vapours attack the granite. The granite decomposes into a mixture of mica, quartz sand and china clay. Lee Moor produces about 20% of England's china clay; the rest comes from St Austell Moor in Cornwall.

The non-porous nature of the granite, plus the high rainfall (over 2000 mm per year), makes Dartmoor suitable for reservoirs. Several of the valleys have been dammed and made into reservoirs to supply Plymouth.

Chalk Landscape

Chalk is a highly permeable rock. Since water drains though chalk, it tends to form uplands (Visual 3). Chalk is also fairly soft, which means that the uplands, or downs, are gently rounded hills. The edge of the downs is marked by a steep slope called a scarp slope. On the other side of the summit, the slope is much more gentle. This gently sloping land is called the dip slope.

There are few rivers or streams on chalk landscapes. There are, however, many dry valleys. The formation of dry valleys is mysterious. They may simply be the result of a wetter climate in the past which caused the water table to be higher. Another theory is that during the Ice Age the chalklands had *permafrost* conditions. Under these conditions all the pores would have been filled with ice Water would therefore have flowed across the surface instead of draining down through the chalk.

Chalk supports only thin, dry and infertile soils. Until the present century, the main type of farming was sheep rearing. The sheep cropped the grass to produce the short turf which was the typical chalk downland. This springy turf is highly suitable for race horses. Several of Britain's most famous race courses and stables (such as Newmarket, Newbury and Epsom) are on the chalklands. However, today's typical chalk downland consists of large fields growing wheat and barley. Water is now piped to the fields. Modern soil conditioners and fertilizers allow the farmer to grow cereals where once only sheep grazed. There are several cement works on or near the chalklands because chalk (or limestone) provides the raw material for the production of cement.

3 The South Downs: a chalk landscape

1 *Write a sentence to explain each of the following: porous rock   pervious rock   impermeable rock.*

2 *Make a copy of Visual 4 which shows a landscape of chalk and clay. Below your diagram copy out the following passage using the correct words:*

> *The landscape consists of ... and ... . The rock type labelled A is ... and the rock type labelled B is ... . The steep slopes are called ... slopes and the more gentle slopes are known as ... slopes. The chalk forms high land because it is ... . There are few ... on chalk landscapes but there are many dry valleys.*

Choose the correct words from this list:
hills valleys permeable streams scarp chalk vales dip clay impermeable.

3 a) *Using Visual 2 to help you, describe the scenery of a granite area.*
  b) *What use can people make of granite landscapes?*

4 a) *What is the landform labelled C on Visual 4?*
  b) *Explain how the landform may have been formed.*

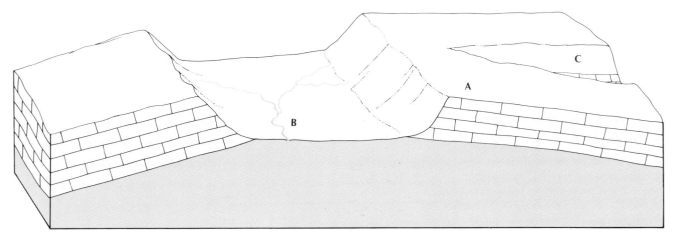

4 A chalk and clay landscape in cross-section

ROCK TYPE AND SCENERY: LIMESTONE

1 Malham, Yorkshire:
a carboniferous limestone landscape

There are several types of limestone, three of which are shown in the table bottom right. They all contain calcium carbonate from the remains of sea shells and coral. They also contain varying amounts of clay, quartz and other minerals which affect their colour. (Another name for calcium carbonate is calcite.)

All the limestones are pervious. Water drains down through joints in the rock. Even the hardest limestone can be dissolved in rainwater. Rainwater is slightly acidic and dissolves calcium carbonate. Water containing dissolved calcium carbonate is called 'hard' water. The dissolved calcium carbonate can come out of solution and be deposited on the inside of kettles and pipes. This 'furring up' reduces their efficiency (Visual 2).

2 Deposit of calcium carbonate inside a kettle

Carboniferous Limestone Scenery
Carboniferous limestone produces very impressive scenery (Visual 1). This kind of limestone is sometimes called 'mountain limestone'. The landscape is dry, with steep slopes and expanses of bare rock. There are few streams and most drainage is underground. The water enlarges the joints and bedding planes in the limestone to create swallow holes and caverns (Visual 4). In the Ingleborough area of North Yorkshire is the huge swallow hole called Gaping Ghyll. Gaping Ghyll is 111 m deep, plunging vertically down into an enormous cavern. Stalactites hang from the roof of the cavern. They are formed by water dripping through the roof and redepositing calcium carbonate. Stalagmites rise from the floor of the cavern. Sometimes a pillar is formed where a stalactite and stalagmite join together. The streams flowing through the cavern emerge where the *water table* reaches the surface as springs.

Name	Colour	Grain size	Hardness	Location
Oolitic	yellow/ brown	small	soft	Cotswolds, Dorset
Magnesian	yellow	large	medium	Durham, Yorkshire
Carboniferous	grey	large	hard	Pennines, Mendips

The land surface is often very irregular. Limestone *pavements* may develop where the soil has been washed away, revealing bare rock. The joints are enlarged by water to form grikes and the upstanding blocks are called clints. There may be deep gorges formed by the collapse of the roof of an underground cavern, or by rapid river erosion in areas where the water table is higher.

The thin, stony soil developed on limestone supports a short, springy pasture. Where the soil is deeper, shrubs and herbs grow, but trees are only found in the valleys. Sheep rearing is the main type of farming.

The landscape lacks trees and is divided into fields bounded by walls. These have been skilfully built of limestone blocks without using any mortar. Such walls are called drystone walls. Isolated buildings on the uplands are often built of the grey limestone and have a solid, cold appearance. Some limestones make very good building stone. Examples are Portland stone, Bath stone and Cotswold stone. Quarrying for building stone or for limestone for cement is an important industry in these areas.

Where limestone scenery is very well developed it is called a 'karst landscape' after the Karst region of Yugoslavia.

1 *How is limestone formed?*

2 *Which constituent of limestone dissolves in rainwater?*

3 *Make a large copy of Visual 3, showing some limestone areas in Britain, and name the areas labelled A to I by choosing from this list:*

Cotswold Hills	*Peak District*	*Purbeck*
Mendip Hills	*Yorkshire Dales*	*Wenlock Edge*
Llangollen	*North York Moors*	*Brecon Beacons*

4 *Study Visual 1. Describe the appearance of the landscape in the photograph. Why does it look like this?*

5 *How might people make use of limestone areas? (Think of farming, industry and tourism.)*

3 Some limestone areas of Britain

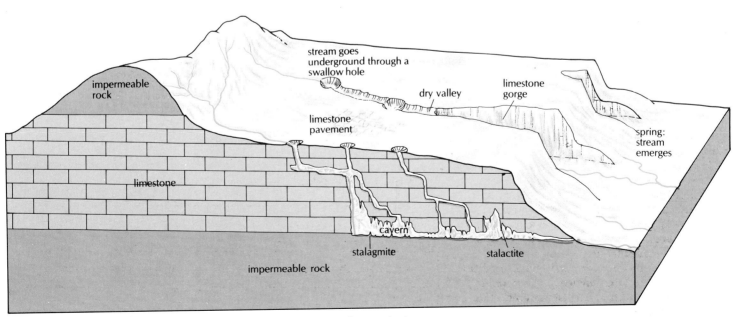

4 Features of a carboniferous limestone landscape

13

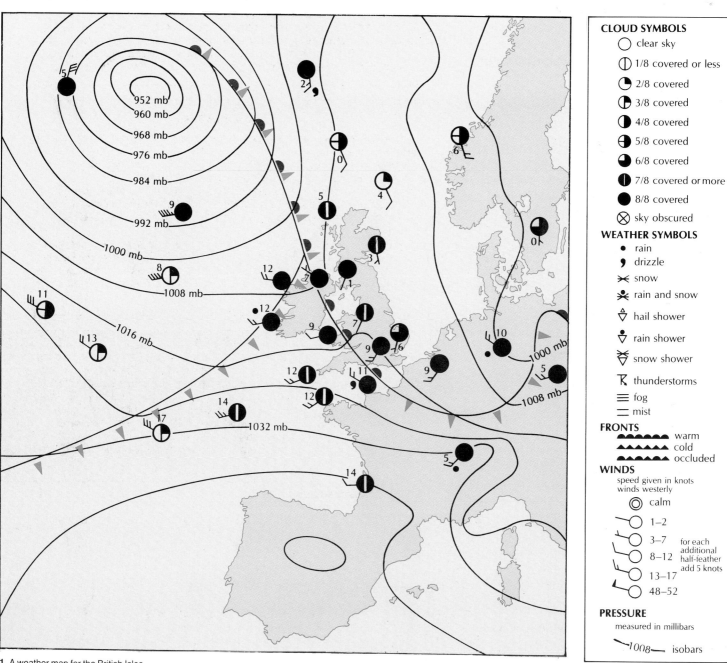

CLOUD SYMBOLS
- ◯ clear sky
- ◑ 1/8 covered or less
- ◔ 2/8 covered
- ◑ 3/8 covered
- ◐ 4/8 covered
- ◕ 5/8 covered
- ◕ 6/8 covered
- ◕ 7/8 covered or more
- ● 8/8 covered
- ⊗ sky obscured

WEATHER SYMBOLS
- • rain
- ، drizzle
- ✳ snow
- ✳ rain and snow
- ▽ hail shower
- ▽ rain shower
- ✳ snow shower
- R thunderstorms
- ≡ fog
- = mist

FRONTS
- ～●～ warm
- ～▲～ cold
- ～▲～ occluded

WINDS
speed given in knots
winds westerly
- ◎ calm
- ◯— 1–2
- ◯⊣ 3–7
- ◯⊣ 8–12   for each additional half-feather add 5 knots
- ◯⊣ 13–17
- ◯⊣ 48–52

PRESSURE
measured in millibars
— *1008* — isobars

1 A weather map for the British Isles

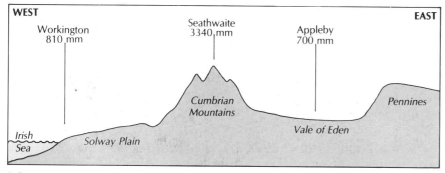

2 Cross-section through the Lake District showing annual rainfall

The weather map (Visual 1) shows another wet day over much of Britain. By studying the key, you will be able to read the symbols which describe the weather at each place on the map.

Weather is the everyday changes in the atmosphere over an area. In Britain the weather conditions change quickly. When we describe the weather over a number of years, we are really talking about climate. Climate can be called the average weather conditions for an area. The most important basic weather processes are outlined in the boxes opposite.

1 Study the weather map and answer the following, using your atlas to help you:

a) Which part of the British Isles has the highest temperature?

b) What is likely to happen to temperatures in western Britain over the next few hours?

c) Which area of Britain has the least cloud?

d) What are the temperature, cloud, wind and pressure conditions in East Anglia?

e) How is the weather in East Anglia likely to change over the next few hours?

2 What is the difference between weather and climate?

3 Study the cross-section (Visual 2) and answer the following:

a) What is the annual rainfall at: i) Workington ii) Seathwaite iii) Appleby?

b) Using information from the boxes, say why this pattern of rainfall happens.

4 Study the boxes and answer the following:

a) What is water vapour?

b) How does the temperature of the air affect the amount of water vapour which the air can hold?

c) Name three ways in which air could be made to rise and cool.

d) What causes differences in atmospheric pressure?

e) What causes winds?

5 Study the climate statistics for Plymouth and Oxford.

a) Draw a graph of the Oxford statistics similar to that shown for Plymouth (Visual 3).

b) Find Plymouth and Oxford in your atlas.

c) What are the January and July temperatures in Plymouth and Oxford? How do you explain the differences?

d) How does the pattern of rainfall differ for the two places? Try to explain the differences.

6 Turn to the page in your atlas showing the climate of the British Isles and answer the following:

a) Find the map showing January temperatures.
   i) Which areas of the British Isles have average January temperatures of over 6 °C?
   ii) Which areas have average January temperatures of below 4 °C?

b) Find the map showing July temperatures.
   i) Which areas of the British Isles have average July temperatures of over 16 °C?
   ii) Which areas have average July temperatures of under 13 °C?

c) What factors appear to affect the pattern of January and July temperatures across the British Isles?

d) Find the map showing annual rainfall over the British Isles.
   i) Name five areas of the British Isles which have over 2000 mm annual rainfall.
   ii) Which areas have less than 750 mm annual rainfall?
   iii) What factors appear to affect the pattern of annual rainfall over the British Isles?

RAINFALL

Water is present in the atmosphere in three forms:
- as a liquid
- as a solid – ice or snow
- as an invisible gas called water vapour.

All air contains water vapour, even in the driest desert. A parcel of air can only hold a certain amount of water vapour. The amount of vapour which the air can hold depends upon its temperature: colder air holds less water vapour than warm air. Warm air rises. As air rises it expands and cools ... as it cools some of the water vapour contained in the air condenses into water droplets ... these water droplets form clouds. The droplets grow bigger and heavier by joining together. Rain will only occur if the tiny cloud droplets become too heavy to remain in the cloud.

TEMPERATURE

Why do temperatures vary from place to place? Among the more important reasons are the following:
- Temperature drops by about 1 °C for every 100 m above sea-level. Hilly and mountainous areas are much colder than nearby lowlands.
- Water heats up more slowly than the land but is able to store the heat longer. This means that in summer the sea is usually cooler than the land, but in winter the sea is warmer than the land. Places near the sea have cooler summers and milder winters than places further inland.
- The angle of the sun's rays affects the temperature. An area receives more heat when the sun shines from a high angle overhead, and less heat when the sun's rays reach it at a low angle. This causes differences between winter and summer temperatures. It also means that places further from the Equator have lower temperatures.

PRESSURE

The air above us is pressing down upon the surface of the Earth. This atmospheric pressure changes from place to place and from time to time. As air rises, this reduces the weight of air at the Earth's surface and creates LOW pressure. As air descends, this increases the weight of the air at the Earth's surface and creates HIGH pressure. Pressure differences are caused by temperature differences: hot air rises, cold air descends. Atmospheric pressure is measured in millibars. Average atmospheric pressure at sea-level is 1013 millibars. Pressure differences between one place and another cause winds. Winds blow from high pressure areas towards areas of low pressure.

CLIMATE STATISTICS FOR PLYMOUTH

Month	J	F	M	A	M	J	J	A	S	O	N	D
Temperature (°C)	7	8	9	10	13	15	17	15	14	12	10	8
Rainfall (mm)	110	75	70	53	60	55	70	72	75	96	105	110

Total rainfall (mm) 951

CLIMATE STATISTICS FOR OXFORD

Month	J	F	M	A	M	J	J	A	S	O	N	D
Temperature (°C)	4	5	8	10	13	15	18	17	14	12	8	5
Rainfall (mm)	65	48	45	50	52	45	60	55	55	60	65	60

Total rainfall (mm) 660

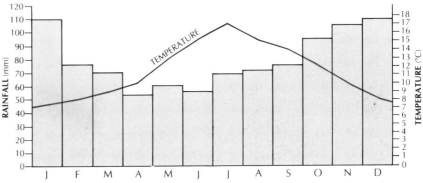

3 Plymouth's climate statistics

The low or depression is the most important weather system affecting Britain. A depression is an area of low pressure. Winds blow in towards the centre of a depression in an anticlockwise direction in the Northern Hemisphere. Depressions bring rain. Visual 1 is a photograph of the North Atlantic taken from a weather satellite. It shows a depression moving from west to east across Britain.

1 a) Where was the centre of the depression when the photograph in Visual 1 was taken?

   b) Which part of Britain was the depression affecting most?

   c) What was the weather like over eastern England?

   d) How do you think that the weather over eastern England would change over the 24 hours after the photograph was taken?

Depressions are huge features, hundreds of kilometres across, which form out over the Atlantic Ocean. Depressions develop where warm air meets cold air. Warm air rises over the colder air to form a warm front. Heavier cold air moves underneath the warm air from behind to form a cold front. It is the changes in position of the two types of air which cause the wind, cloud and rain associated with a depression, as Visual 2 explains. The depression moves eastwards taking its winds and rain with it. As a depression passes overhead, a place will have a sequence of weather, mostly wet and windy!

The warm air (the warm sector of the depression) gradually rises higher until it loses contact with the ground. The warm and cold fronts join to form an occluded front, and the depression quickly fades.

Anticyclones

An anticyclone is an area of high pressure. Anticyclones are less common than depressions in Britain. This is why long periods of settled, fine weather are rare in Britain. Winds blow outwards from the centre of an anticylone in a clockwise direction. The weather in an anticylone varies according to the season:

◦ In the summer anticyclones bring hot, sunny, dry weather. If an anticyclone remains over Britain during the summer for more than a few days, we speak of a 'heat-wave'.

◦ In winter, however, the weather can be much less pleasant. Since there are few clouds with an anticyclone, the Earth's heat escapes quickly at night. This causes frost on the ground and it becomes very cold. Winter anticyclones often have

1 Satellite view of a depression approaching Britain

fog. The cold ground causes water vapour in the lower air to condense into droplets. These hang in the air until the heat of the sun raises the temperature. The fog may hang around all day because of the weak winter sun.

2 a) What is: i) a front   ii) a depression
       iii) an anticyclone?

   b) How does a depression develop?

3 What weather would you expect in the following stages of a depression:

   a) As the warm front passes overhead?

   b) In the warm sector?

   c) As the cold front passes overhead?

4 How and why does the weather in an anticyclone vary between winter and summer?

5 Visual 1 (on page 14) shows the symbols used on official weather maps.

   a) Visual 4 shows the weather recorded at three weather stations, as shown by the official weather symbols. Fully describe the weather at each station.

   b) The three weather stations are sited near one another. A depression is passing over them. At which stage of the depression do you think each station is located?

6 Draw a weather station located under the centre of an anticyclone in: a) June   b) January.

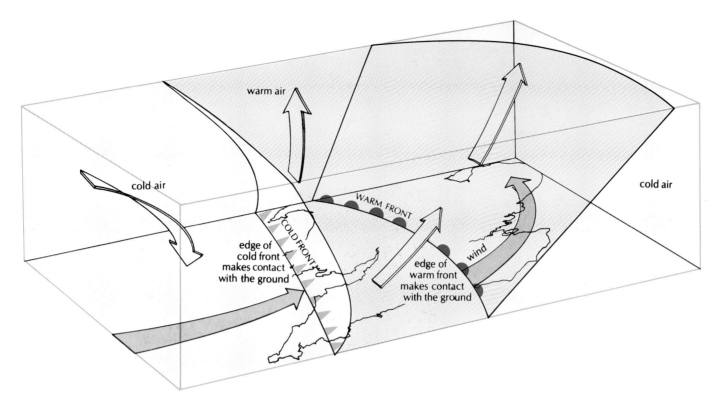

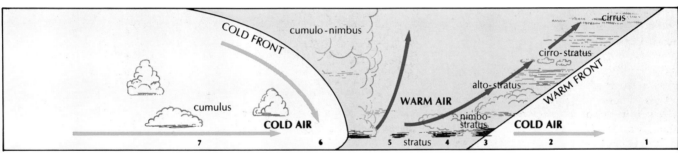

7 The depression has passed. In the cold sector it is bright and sunny, but cool.

6 The cold front passes. Temperature falls. Huge cumulo-nimbus clouds may form, bringing very heavy showers and even thunderstorms.

5 In the warm sector it is warm with low stratus cloud and showers.

4 The warm front passes. Temperature rises and it rains steadily.

3 Thick nimbo-stratus clouds pass overhead. It starts to rain as the warm front approaches.

2 Thicker clouds form lower in the sky.

1 The first sign of the approaching depression is cirrus cloud, high in the sky.

Overall direction of movement is from left to right

2 A depression in three dimensions (top diagram) and in cross-section (bottom diagram). See also Visual 3

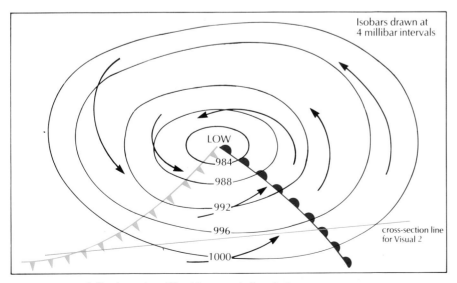

3 The depression of Visual 2 represented in a chart

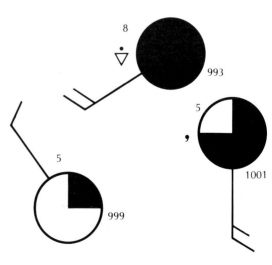

4 The weather recorded at three stations

17

This Green and Pleasant Land?

Seen from the air, England is no longer green. The parched, brown landscape sweats through another sweltering day. The grass has shrivelled, the flowers have withered and died.

INDUSTRY HIT by GREAT DROUGHT

The drought is costing British industry millions of pounds. Water is the universal raw material. A spokesman for a large Lincolnshire food freezing factory said "We're spending £50,000 to recirculate water. Without it we could lose most of our products.

THE TAPS ARE SWITCHED OFF. In some parts of South West England and Wales the mains water to peoples' homes has been switched off. The unfortunate residents have had to use stand pipes placed in the street. Queues for water have become a common sight.

Drought threatens FOOD SHORTAGES

We can look forward to a dramatic reduction in the numbers of British-grown vegetables. With a continuing dry summer the situation will become catastrophic.

There is a saying about Britain's weather which is much used by Americans visiting the country: 'If you don't like the weather, stick around – it'll change within the hour. There is a lot of truth in that saying. Britain's weather is very varied. Fourteen days without rain is rare; if it happens an official drought is declared. In 1976 there was the worst drought for 500 years. Week after week of hot, sunny weather gave Britain a Mediterranean-style summer. Wonderful weather! But the drought caused many problems.

What Caused It?

Parts of southern England had less than a quarter of their average rainfall during the year from October 1975 to September 1976. The very dry winter and spring of 1975–76 meant that the reservoirs were already low before the drought began. The main cause of this lack of rainfall was an anticyclone over Britain. This deflected depressions to the north and south of Britain. Such an anticyclone is called a 'blocking high'. Fortunately the blocking high faded away in September and the last few months of 1976 had heavy rain.

Why Is Britain's Weather So Variable?

The passage of depressions across the country has a lot to do with Britain's variable weather. As we saw on the pages 16 and 17, a depression brings cloud, rain and changing temperatures, and clear weather after it has passed. During the winter Britain receives a series of depressions. During the summer the depressions usually track across Norway.

Another important factor in the changeability of Britain's weather is the type of air mass which affects the country. An air mass is a large body of air which has the same temperature and *humidity* throughout. It is formed when air lies over an area of land or sea for long enough to pick up the heat and moisture from that area. The area where the air mass forms is called the source region. Four major air masses affect Britain (Visual 2).

1 An advertisement from the National Water Council (1976)

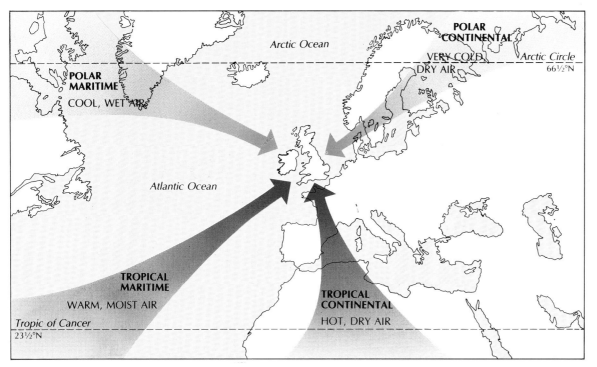

2 Air masses affecting the British Isles

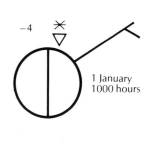

1 January
1000 hours

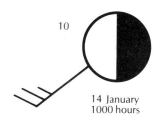

14 January
1000 hours

3 Heat-wave in the city

4 Snowstorm in the city

27 January
1000 hours

5 Three weather records

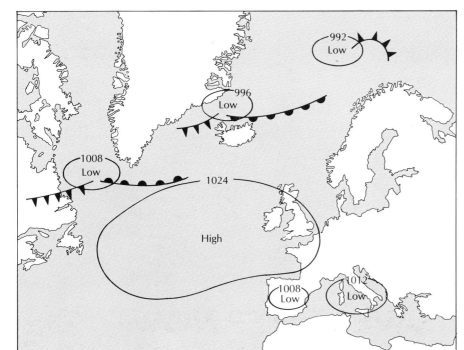

6 The weather conditions in June 1976

1 a) List five effects of the 1976 drought.

  b) In which months was the drought at its worst?

  c) Describe five ways of saving water at home.

2 Ask your parents about the 1976 drought. What can they remember about the drought?

3 Study Visual 6. How does this weather map help to explain the cause of the 1976 drought?

4 a) What is an air mass?

  b) What is the source region of an air mass?

  c) Copy Visual 2.

  d) Why do air masses change when they move away from their source regions?

5 Visual 5 shows the weather recorded at a British weather station during January, as shown by the official weather symbols (see page 14).

  a) Fully describe the weather on each day.

  b) Which air mass do you think is affecting the weather on each day shown?

  c) Draw three more diagrams showing the weather at the station during July, when the following air masses affect the weather: i) Tropical Continental
  ii) Tropical Maritime   iii) Polar Maritime.

1 Rain stops play

2 Motorway accident in fog

3 The shipwreck of the Athina-B on Brighton beach

Rain stopped play: a sadly familiar phrase for cricket fans in Britain. But it is not just sport that is affected by our weather!

At Home
Despite the fact that many of us live centrally heated, indoor lives protected from the weather, we are still affected by it. Our clothes and our heating bills depend to a large extent on the weather. Frost may burst pipes by freezing the water in them. High winds may remove roof tiles and blow down fences. Storms are more common in Britain than many people think. In 1984 a *tornado* swept through the Nottinghamshire village of Cotham and demolished several houses. Tornadoes are estimated to occur on an average of 31 days a year!

Transport
A little snow often brings Britain sliding to a halt. Frost and black ice cause many accidents. Councils spend millions of pounds on gritting and salting roads to overcome ice. Snow and ice can close airports and slow down railways. Fog can cause road accidents (Visual 2) and close airports. Strong winds create problems for high-sided vehicles; bridges may be closed to such vehicles on windy days. Storms pose danger for shipping. Every year many people are drowned when their ships are wrecked around Britain's coasts (Visual 3).

Farming
Farming is greatly influenced by the weather. The wetter western areas of Britain have a mild climate, favouring the growth of grass and dairy farming. It is too wet for arable farming. In eastern England the drier climate favours arable crops. East Anglia has become the 'bread basket' of Britain with its huge fields of wheat. Sprinkler irrigation is needed most years in the drier eastern parts.

The length of the growing season is shown by Visual 4. Farmers in Cornwall and Dyfed can grow early flowers and vegetables well before the rest of Britain. In northern Britain, however, the shorter growing season means that many crops such as wheat will not ripen.

High winds and heavy showers can damage crops. Livestock farmers can lose their animals in snow drifts. Late spring frosts are feared by fruit farmers since they can kill fruit blossom. The weather can 'make or break' a farmer.

Water Supply

The heavy rainfall of north and west Britain provides a much needed surplus to meet the water needs of the more densely populated but drier south and east. Reservoirs in the Pennines and the Lake District supply water by pipeline and river to the water deficient areas. Periods of heavy rain or short downpours can cause serious flooding (see page 34). Serious droughts are rare in Britain but they cause problems when they do occur.

Leisure

Cricket clubs lose money when rain prevents play. Skiing areas lose money when it does not snow. Canal locks are closed during drought, preventing cruising. Britain's seaside resorts welcome long sunny spells, but these are all too rare. Many British tourists prefer to sunbathe on Mediterranean beaches where sunshine is almost guaranteed. If a long sunny spell does occur, the roads to the coast and to major inland tourist attractions become heavily congested. Beaches and promenades become crowded and the resorts' facilities are heavily over-used. Visual 5 shows that it is the southern resorts which benefit most from long hours of sunshine.

1 How has the weather affected you over the past week? Compare your answer with that of your neighbour.

2 Make a list of ten ways in which the weather might affect you: a) in the winter   b) in the summer.

3 How does the weather affect transport?

4 Explain the following statements:

  a) Arable farming is difficult in the west of Britain.

  b) Farmers in Cornwall and Dyfed can grow early flowers and vegetables well before the rest of Britain.

  c) In eastern England sprinkler irrigation is needed in most years.

5 What are the advantages and disadvantages to a British seaside resort of a long sunny spell during August?

6 Using an atlas to help you, write down the length of the growing season in the following places:

Southampton   Aberdeen   Fort William   Pembroke Oxford   Plymouth   Leeds.

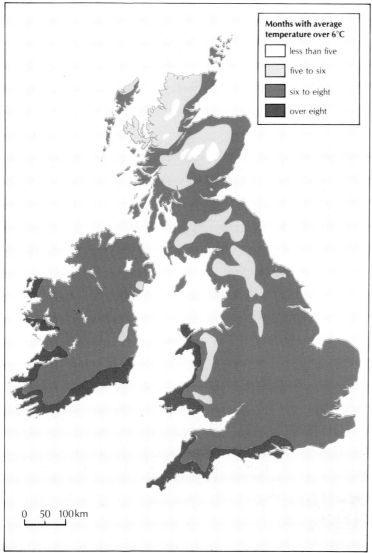

Months with average temperature over 6°C
- less than five
- five to six
- six to eight
- over eight

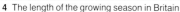

0   50   100km

4 The length of the growing season in Britain

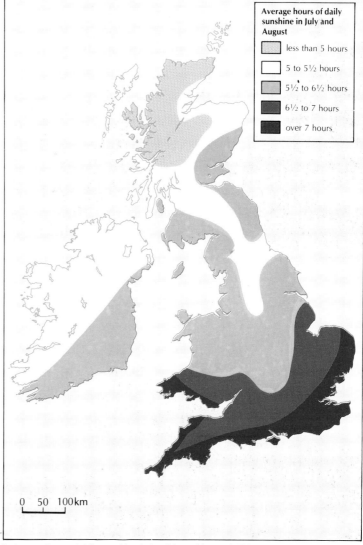

Average hours of daily sunshine in July and August
- less than 5 hours
- 5 to 5½ hours
- 5½ to 6½ hours
- 6½ to 7 hours
- over 7 hours

0   50   100km

5 Average hours of daily sunshine during July and August in Britain

ASSIGNMENT ONE
Britain's Climate

As a nation we seem obsessed by the weather. It is probably our most common topic of conservation. We use the word 'weather' to describe what conditions are like on a particular day (the temperature, rainfall, cloud, wind and so on).

Weather varies from place to place and from time to time. It is difficult to make general statements about the weather because it changes so much. Weather records, however, go back over many years. By consulting these, we can get a fair idea of the normal pattern of weather for a particular place. This idea of the average weather we call 'climate'.

Your Assignment
You work for the Meteorological Office, in a small team of four. Your assignment is based on the memo sent to you by your marketing manager. You are asked to look more closely at the climate of Britain.

° Consider how the climate varies in different parts of Britain.
° What are the main reasons for this variety?

Resources
1 DATA FILE.
2 The Meteorological Office memo.
3 The map of Britain.
4 Climate maps, graphs and statistics in your atlas.

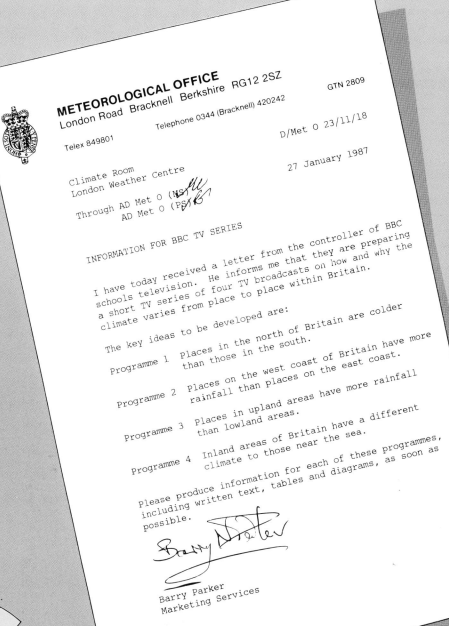

METEOROLOGICAL OFFICE
London Road Bracknell Berkshire RG12 2SZ

GTN 2809

Telephone 0344 (Bracknell) 420242

Telex 849801

D/Met O 23/11/18

27 January 1987

Climate Room
London Weather Centre

Through AD Met O (MS)
AD Met O (PS)

INFORMATION FOR BBC TV SERIES

I have today received a letter from the controller of BBC schools television. He informs me that they are preparing a short TV series of four TV broadcasts on how and why the climate varies from place to place within Britain.

The key ideas to be developed are:

Programme 1 Places in the north of Britain are colder than those in the south.

Programme 2 Places on the west coast of Britain have more rainfall than places on the east coast.

Programme 3 Places in upland areas have more rainfall than lowland areas.

Programme 4 Inland areas of Britain have a different climate to those near the sea.

Please produce information for each of these programmes, including written text, tables and diagrams, as soon as possible.

Barry Parker
Marketing Services

	Jan	Feb	Mar	Apr	May	Jun	Jul	Aug	Sep	Oct	Nov	Dec		
FALMOUTH 51 m above sea-level														
Temperature (°C)	7	8	9	11	12	15	16	15	14	12	10	9	Range of temperature	9 °C
Rainfall (mm)	121	98	77	65	66	45	71	75	76	108	121	128	Total rainfall	1051 mm
EASTBOURNE 11 m above sea-level														
Temperature (°C)	5	6	8	10	12	15	18	17	15	12	9	7	Range of temperature	13 °C
Rainfall (mm)	76	52	48	50	44	40	52	56	62	82	103	80	Total rainfall	745 mm
SOUTHEND-ON-SEA 5 m above sea-level														
Temperature (°C)	4	5	7	9	12	16	18	18	16	12	8	5	Range of temperature	14 °C
Rainfall (mm)	48	36	33	41	41	34	51	50	40	56	61	48	Total rainfall	539 mm
MANCHESTER 38 m above sea-level														
Temperature (°C)	6	6	7	9	12	14	16	16	14	11	8	6	Range of temperature	10 °C
Rainfall (mm)	88	70	49	53	66	64	80	87	74	95	88	76	Total rainfall	890 mm
NEWCASTLE UPON TYNE 22 m above sea-level														
Temperature (°C)	5	5	6	8	10	13	15	14	12	10	7	6	Range of temperature	10 °C
Rainfall (mm)	55	42	40	43	48	42	74	75	52	55	54	55	Total rainfall	635 mm
FORT WILLIAM 54 m above sea-level														
Temperature (°C)	5	5	7	8	10	13	14	13	12	10	7	5	Range of temperature	9 °C
Rainfall (mm)	248	181	130	124	108	120	133	155	176	231	197	221	Total rainfall	2024 mm
ELGIN 17 m above sea-level														
Temperature (°C)	3	5	6	8	11	13	15	14	13	10	6	4	Range of temperature	12 °C
Rainfall (mm)	58	44	43	48	53	52	74	72	68	74	57	50	Total rainfall	693 mm

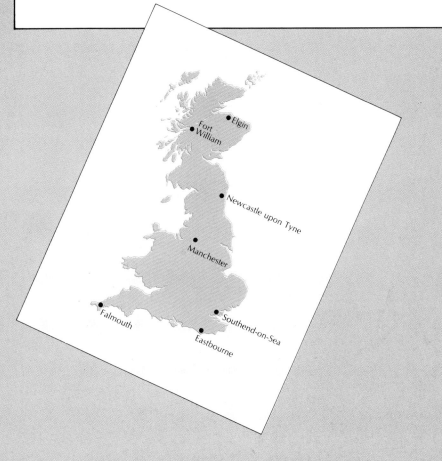

Work Programme

You should work in groups of four.

1 a) Read the memo from your marketing manager.
  b) Discuss the memo and make sure that you understand it.

2 Take each programme in turn. Discuss the theme of the programme. Do you agree with the key idea? If so, why?

3 Use the information shown here, and any other resources, to construct a series of visuals which help to explain each programme's key idea. These could include bar graphs and scatter graphs, isoline maps, diagrams, cartoons, newspaper cuttings, ideas for interviews and programme locations.

4 For each key idea, prepare a written summary. This should say why and to what extent each key idea is true. Use the visuals you have produced.

5 Think of a suitable, catchy title for each programme.

6 When the work on each programme has been finished, assemble your final report for handing in.

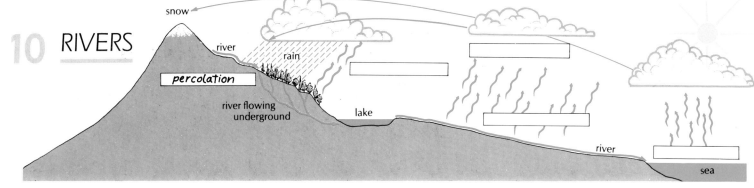

1 The hydrological cycle

It is cold and wet for much of the time in the highlands of Fforest Fawr in the Brecon Beacons National Park. The landscape is bleak moorland with steep hills and mountains rising to over 700 m. The dark masses of Fan Nedd and Fan Llia brood somberly over the valley of the Afon Llia. From these mountain slopes flow dozens of rivulets and streams. They flow to the valley floor where they enter the larger stream known as Afon Llia. The area from which a stream, such as Afon Llia, receives its water is called its drainage basin or catchment.

An average of 2200 mm of rain falls each year on these mountains. The rainfall and the flow of the stream are part of the hydrological cycle (Visual 1). This is the name given to the movement of water between the sea, the air and the land. Water evaporates from the sea and the land, forms clouds, falls to the ground as rain or snow, and evaporates again … . This cycle has no beginning and no end.

When rain starts to fall it drains into the soil. If the rain is heavy, much of the water will stand on the surface forming small pools in hollows on the ground. When the hollows are full, water will begin to run downhill as overland flow. The rocks of the upper drainage basin of the Afon Llia are old red sandstone which is semipermeable. As a result there are many tributaries flowing into the Afon Llia.

We can think of the river as a system. The output of the system, the river's flow, depends upon how much input of water there has been. The input depends upon how much rain has fallen and how much of it has been lost by evaporation and *transpiration* (the water taken up and lost by plants). These are often considered together as evapo-transpiration. Evapo-transpiration is highest on hot, sunny days and lowest on cold, cloudy days.

The relative importance of the inputs of water to the river can be measured and the results put into an equation called the *water balance equation* (see the large box on the opposite page).

Looking at the area of the River Neath (into which the Afon Llia flows), we can see how much water is lost by evapo-transpiration in a full year:

Precipitation (rain and snow):	1650 mm
River output (discharge):	1220 mm
Evapo-transpiration:	430 mm

This means that 73% of the water which fell on the River Neath drainage basin flowed out along the river. This is a high percentage. In eastern England the percentage may be below 20%. What causes such great differences in the water balance? One or more of these reasons may be important for any particular drainage basin:

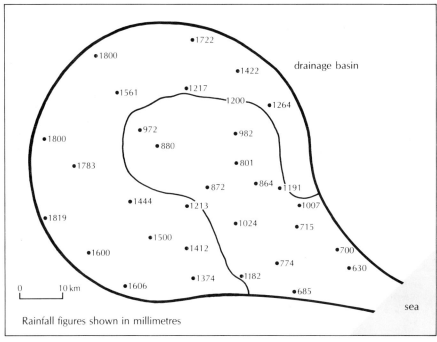

2 Rainfall figures recorded across a drainage basin

° The climate of the catchment area. Evapo-transpiration rates are much higher in the east of England, where temperatures are higher and there are many more hours of sunshine.
° The geology. A drainage basin of permeable rocks will lose more water to storage. Rainfall will soak into, or through, the rocks and remain as ground water.
° The soil cover. Areas with thin soil cover, such as the Brecon Beacons, will have rapid runoff. The more soil, the more rain is soaked up by the soil.
° The vegetation. Plants intercept rainfall and reduce the amount of water going into streams and rivers. Forested areas also have much higher rates of evapo-transpiration than moorland or grassland.
° The slope. The steeper the slope, the more rain flows downhill. On flatter land rain is more likely to soak into the soil and rocks.
° Human action. Water may be withdrawn from the river for water supply purposes. Waste water and sewage may be added to the river. Land drains in farmland will increase the flow of water into rivers, as will sewers and drains in urban areas. Large expanses of concrete, such as car parks, may trap more water. This will then be lost through evapo-transpiration.

1 Write a sentence to explain each of these terms:
 a) precipitation   b) drainage basin   c) overland flow
 d) evapo-transpiration.

2 Copy the diagram in Visual 1 (the hydrological cycle) and write suitable labels in the empty boxes.

3 Visual 2 shows the rainfall figures recorded across a drainage basin.

  a) Copy the map.

  b) Draw on isohyets at 200 mm intervals. The 1200 mm isohyet has been drawn for you. An isohyet is a line joining places with equal rainfall.

  c) Write a paragraph to describe the pattern of rainfall revealed by the isohyets. What might cause this pattern?

4 The situation of four different drainage basins is described below.

  a) Which do you think would have the highest output or discharge? Explain your reasons.

  b) Which would have the lowest discharge? Again, explain your reasons.

  c) Which basin would have the highest rate of evapo-transpiration?

  d) Which basin would hold most water in the rocks?

DRAINAGE BASIN A
Mountain area (Lake District) – moorland with some forest; high rainfall (2000 mm+ per year); thin soil; mainly impermeable rock.

DRAINAGE BASIN B
Lowland area (Essex) – farmland with large town; low rainfall (700 mm per year); deep soil; mainly impermeable rock.

DRAINAGE BASIN C
Hilly area (Wiltshire) – chalk downland; thin soil; cereal farming on flatter ground, sheep on steeper slopes.

DRAINAGE BASIN D
Urban area (West Midlands) – gently undulating lowland; industrial city.

5 a) What is the water balance?

The table below shows the rainfall and river discharge statistics for the River Ystwyth in west Wales over a water year:

  b) Calculate: i) the total rainfall   ii) the total discharge.

  c) What percentage of the total rainfall ran off as river discharge?

  d) Draw line graphs to illustrate the statistics in the table.

  e) Explain the patterns revealed by the line graphs.

MONTH	Oct	Nov	Dec	Jan	Feb	Mar	Apr	May	Jun	Jul	Aug	Sep
RAINFALL (mm)	76	122	341	64	149	80	85	109	127	115	60	90
DISCHARGE (mm)	62	70	356	73	98	49	44	47	61	33	37	34

MEASURING THE WATER BALANCE OF A DRAINAGE BASIN

1 Rainfall is measured using a rain gauge. The water collected in the bottle is poured into a specially calibrated measuring cylinder which registers rainfall in mm. In order to gain an accurate figure for rainfall, several rain gauges must be used across the drainage basin. If enough gauges are used, isohyets (lines joining points of equal rainfall) can be drawn on a map of the drainage basin.

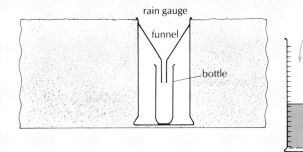

2 Evapo-transpiration can be measured using a *lysimeter*. A column of soil is cut and placed inside a container such as an oil drum. This is then inserted into the hole in the ground. The rainfall is measured and the flow of water through the lysimeter is trapped in the lower can. The amount of water stored within the soil can be calculated by weighing the upper can (1 ml of water weighs 1 g). The amount of evapo-transpiration can then be found by using the following formula:

output = rainfall − evapo-transpiration − storage

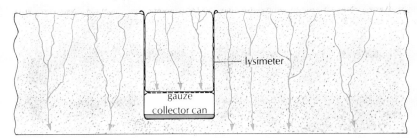

3 River flow can be measured using a current meter. This measures the velocity of the river. The amount of water passing through the river channel (or discharge) can be calculated using the following formula:

discharge = velocity × cross-sectional area

It is rather more fun to measure discharge by using an orange. The orange is thrown into the river and the time taken for it to travel along a measured section is recorded. A number of runs are made and an average time obtained. The orange is a suitable float because it is highly visible. Also it floats just beneath the surface of the water so that there is no wind interference. The orange can also be eaten afterwards, of course! More sophisticated methods of measuring discharge include *weirs* and flumes. Flumes are artificial channels of known cross-sectional area built into the river bed. Since the area is known only the depth of water need be obtained in order to calculate the discharge. Some flumes are continuously monitored by computer.

4 The water balance equation is now used as follows: Put the figures for precipitation and evapo-transpiration into the water balance equation to check the answers and find out how much water is stored within the basin:

river discharge = precipitation − evapo-transpiration ± storage

The water balance in Britain is usually calculated over a period of 12 months running from 1 October to 30 September. This is called the water year. This period is chosen because the end of the summer is the time when least water is stored within the drainage basin.

11 RIVERS: THE LONG PROFILE

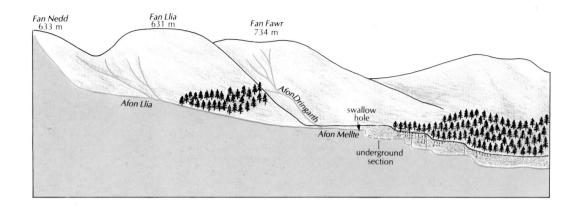

1 The course of the Afon Llia and Afon Mellte

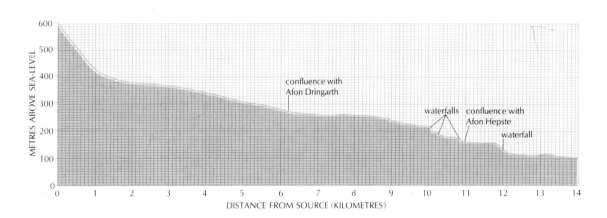

2 The long profile of the Afon Llia and Afon Mellte

3 A model long profile

Visual 1 shows the course of the Afon Llia. This is a view from the source of the Afon Llia to the point where it joins a larger river (the River Neath), at Pontneddfechan.

Visual 2 shows the height of the river above sea-level, plotted against distance from its source. This is the longitudinal, or long profile. As with most rivers, the Afon Llia has an uneven long profile. In some places it is steep, in others much less steep. The Afon Llia even has a point where the water disappears underground for a while. This occurs where the water flows over highly permeable limestone.

A simplified, or ideal, form of long profile is shown in Visual 3. Few rivers would have a long profile as smooth as this, but we can use it as a *model* to compare with the long profiles of real rivers. As the next few pages will show, the work which a river does – the amount of erosion and deposition – usually changes at different points along a river's long profile.

The appearance of the river valley is largely due to the action of the river itself, and the weathering on the slopes above the river. The river erodes the rocks of its valley, transporting the debris and later depositing it.

The amount of erosion depends upon the speed of water flow, the amount of material carried and the type of rock over which the river flows. Soft rocks are eroded much more quickly than strong and resistant rocks. The box below lists the ways in which a river erodes.

Most of the time little erosion actually occurs. It is during times of flood that most erosion happens. The increased input of water means that the river has much more energy. The discharge will greatly increase and the river will be able to carry much more material. Even large boulders can be swept along, crashing against the bed and banks of the channel. As the river loses energy, the flood subsides and much material is deposited by the river.

A RIVER ERODES IN SEVERAL WAYS:

- The running water itself may carry away the loose material.
- The rocks and pebbles carried by the river crash against the sides and bed of the channel and remove more material. This is called corrasion.
- The rocks and pebbles carried by the river crash into each other and break up into smaller fragments. This is called attrition.
- The water can dissolve the minerals in some rocks, for example the calcium carbonate in chalk and limestone. This is called solution.

---

1 Write a sentence to explain what these words mean:
   a) attrition   b) corrasion   c) solution.

2 Using the Ordnance Survey map extract (Visual 4), what do the symbols at the following grid references represent:
   931152   926193   935155   925128   946137?

3 a) Why does the Afon Mellte disappear underground at grid reference 928124?

   b) What is the name of the feature in the river bed where the Afon Mellte goes underground?

   c) Why does the Afon Mellte reappear at the surface at grid reference 927122?

4 How does the Afon Dringarth differ from the Afon Llia?

5 What facilities are there for tourists along the valley of the Afon Llia and Afon Mellte?

6 What evidence is there that the valley of the Afon Llia has been used by people in the past?

7 a) Using the Ordnance Survey map extract, draw the long profile of the Afon Dringarth. Visual 2 should help you.

   b) How does the long profile of the Afon Dringarth compare with that of the Afon Llia? Can you explain any differences?

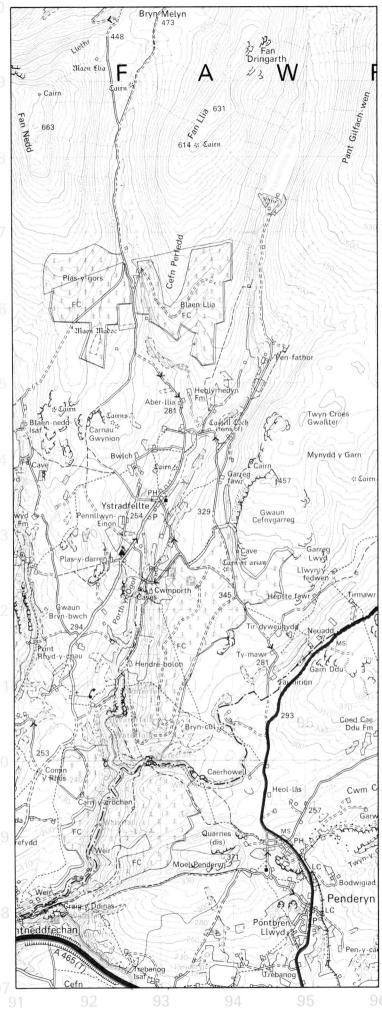

4 Extract from the Ordnance Survey map of the Brecon Beacons (scale 1:50 000)

The Torrent Stage

Visual 1 shows the Afon Llia flowing in its upper or *torrent* stage. The valley sides are steep, giving a V-shaped cross-section. The river's course is not straight. It flows around interlocking spurs of higher land. The river is eroding rapidly downwards and transporting large amounts of material downriver. The shape of the river's valley was changed by a glacier, which moved down the valley during the Ice Age.

The Valley Stage

Visual 2 shows the Afon Llia flowing across a broad area of flat land called the *flood plain*. The river's course is marked by a series of curves called meanders. Visual 3 shows how the main force of the river's flow is concentrated on the outside of the meander. Erosion is greatest on the outside of the meander, while some deposition takes place on the inside. Visual 4 shows a well developed river cliff and slip off slope (river beach) on the Afon Llia. This lateral erosion removes the interlocking spurs and forms the flood plain.

In its valley stage, a river is in a state of balance. The input of water and sediment equals the output of water and sediment. There is deposition as well as erosion in this section, but the deposition is only temporary. Sooner or later the sediment will be eroded and transported further downriver.

The Afon Mellte flows over four spectacular waterfalls in its valley stage (Visual 7). The waterfalls have been caused by faulting, where the rock has been cracked by pressure or tension. This has shifted the rock layers, causing softer shale to be brought into the river's course. The river has rapidly eroded the shale, creating a waterfall (Visual 8). At the foot of the waterfall is a deep section called the plunge pool. Two of the waterfalls have overhangs at the top. This is caused by water splashing back on to the softer shale and eroding it. In one waterfall the shale has been eroded back so far that it is possible to walk behind the waterfall and look at the curtain of falling water. Eventually the overhanging rock will collapse into the plunge pool. The undercutting will then start again. A series of collapses causes the position of the waterfall to move slowly upstream. A narrow, steep-sided *gorge* is left (Visual 5).

1 The Afon Llia in its torrent stage

2 The flood plain of the Afon Llia

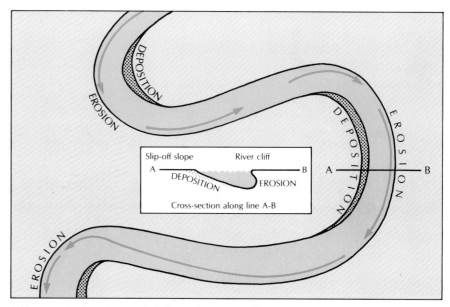

3 How meanders form: the arrow indicates maximum current flow

4 A river cliff and slip off slope on the Afon Llia

1 Study Visuals 1 and 2. Describe the scene in each photograph. How does the appearance of the river and its valley vary between the two?

2 In your own words say what the following are:
a) meander   b) lateral erosion   c) flood plain.

3 Study Visual 4.

a) Make a sketch of the photograph and label the features which you can see.

b) How have these features been formed?

4 a) Copy Visual 8.

b) Why does the top of the waterfall overhang?

c) Why is there a plunge pool beneath the waterfall?

d) Below the waterfall, the river valley is narrow with steep sides. What is this type of valley called and how has it been formed?

5 Study Visual 6. What does it show about a river in its valley stage?

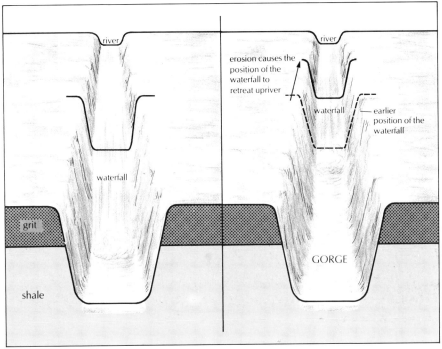

5 How a gorge forms

7 Waterfalls on the Afon Mellte

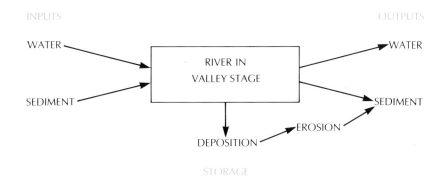

6 Flow diagram showing a river in its valley stage

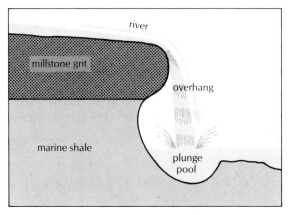

8 A waterfall in cross-section

1 The River Neath entering Swansea Bay

Below the fourth waterfall, the Afon Mellte joins the River Neath at Pontneddfechan. The river meanders down to the sea and its flood plain becomes wider. Over hundreds of years the river constantly changes course as meanders are cut off to form *ox bow lakes* (Visual 2). The ox bow lakes will eventually fill with sediment and dry up. At this stage, the river's profile is almost flat. In its last 12 km, the River Neath descends only 12 m; in its first 12 km, the Afon Llia descends over 450 m! The river is now so close to sea-level that the process of vertical erosion has almost stopped.

The River Neath enters the sea through a broad tidal inlet called an estuary. Visual 1 shows the Neath entering Swansea Bay. Notice the broad expanse of mudflats deposited in the estuary. Many British rivers enter the sea through estuaries. Some, such as the Thames Estuary, are very wide. The lower reaches of some rivers have been drowned by a rise in sea-level. A drowned river valley is called a ria. An example is the estuary of the River Tamar at Plymouth. The sea runs inland along the former river valley, forming a narrow, deep sea inlet. In south east England such drowned river valleys are called creeks.

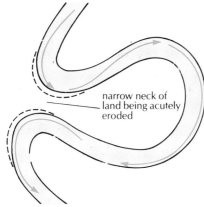

narrow neck of land being acutely eroded

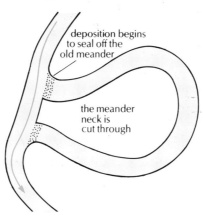

deposition begins to seal off the old meander

the meander neck is cut through

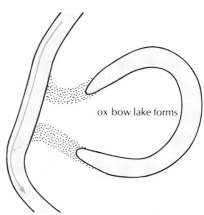

ox bow lake forms

2 How an ox bow lake is formed

CHANGES IN SEA-LEVEL

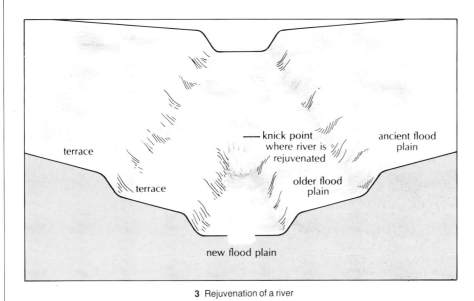

3 Rejuvenation of a river

When the sea-level rises (or falls) the river's long profile is affected. When the sea-level rises, the lower sections of the river will be drowned by sea water. Drowned river valleys are called rias or creeks.

When the sea-level falls, the process of rejuvenation happens. Some waterfalls and rapids are the result of this process. Rejuvenation means to make young again – to restore youth. How can a river be made youthful again? A fall in sea-level will cause the river to flow faster and erode downwards more quickly. The river will cut into the flood plain and create a new flood plain at a lower level. Given enough time, the river could remove the old flood plain completely, but often the sea-level changes again before this can happen. As a result, there may be a series of terraces rising above the present flood plain marking the positions of earlier flood plains. These terraces are very useful to people since they provide flat land close to the river but above flood-level. Such terraces make ideal sites for villages.

THE RIVER AND PEOPLE

4 The Maen Llia standing stone

The Afon Llia has been a routeway for thousands of years. Visual 4 shows the prehistoric standing stone called Maen Llia. Running near Maen Llia is a track which marks the course of Sarn Helen, the Roman road running from the fort at Brecon Gaer to the fort at Nidum near Neath.

In its upper reaches (over 400 m above sea-level) the Afon Llia is marshy moorland, but rough grazing for sheep soon appears as you travel down the valley. Sheep pens are the first sign of human building. At a height of about 370 m the first trees grow – a coniferous plantation. The Forestry Commission have built a picnic area with wooden tables and benches beside the river, a sign of the increasing use of the valley by tourists. Fenced fields, enclosing improved grazing for sheep and cattle, appear below 330 m. The first farm in the valley is at a height of 280 m. Just below the farm is the confluence of the Afon Llia and the Afon Dringarth. The valley of the Afon Dringarth has been dammed to create Ystradfellte Reservoir. This 24 hectare reservoir supplies the water needs of the coastal towns. The reservoir stores 3200 million litres of water.

In its lower reaches, the River Neath supplies cooling water to a range of industries built along its flood plain. The river is navigable for small coasters as far as Neath. The derelict Neath Canal was once used by barges as far as Glyn Neath. Today heavy traffic speeds along the A465 dual carriageway, which follows the valley of the Neath down to the sea.

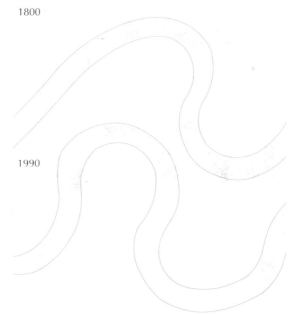

1800

1990

5 Changes in a river's course

1 a) *Copy the diagrams in Visual 5.*

   b) *Add labels to the diagrams explaining the changes which will have happened between 1800 and 1990.*

   c) *Draw a third labelled diagram to show what might happen to the meander within the next 200 years.*

2 *List six uses of the Afon Llia and/or River Neath.*

3 a) *How far does the River Neath descend over its last 12 km?*

   b) *How far does the Afon Llia descend over its first 12 km?*

   c) *How can you explain the difference?*

4 a) *What is meant by rejuvenation?*

   b) *How can a river be rejuvenated?*

   c) *What are terraces and why are they useful to people?*

ASSIGNMENT TWO
River Studies Fieldwork Exercises

The most useful piece of information to gather is the amount of water flowing through the river channel. This is known as the 'discharge'. Water authorities need to know the discharge of a river, before they can divert water for water supply purposes.

Your Assignment
- Calculate the discharge of the Afon Llia from the fieldwork measurements provided.
- Conduct your own fieldwork measurements of a stream, in order to calculate its discharge.

METHOD
Fieldwork Measurements
1 Choose a straight section of the stream with an even width and measure a 10 m distance along the bank. Place a marker pole at the beginning and end of the 10 m.
2 Measure the width of the stream at the water level.
3 Using the metre ruler, measure the depth of water at 50 cm distances across the stream.
4 Drop an orange into the stream above the first marker. Note the time, in seconds, that the orange takes to travel the 10 m. This should be repeated ten times in order to obtain an average time. The orange should be dropped into the water at different points across the stream.

Discharge Calculations
1 Plot the width and depth measurements on graph paper. This produces an accurate cross-sectional drawing of the stream channel.
2 Calculate the area of the channel (A) by counting up the squares of graph paper covered by the stream channel.
3 Add up the ten times taken by the orange to travel the 10 m distance and calculate the average time (T).
4 Divide ten by the average time; this gives you the velocity (V) in metres per second.
5 Multiply the velocity by the cross-sectional area to get the discharge in cubic metres per second (cumecs).
6 Multiply the discharge by 0.8. (The orange floats near the surface, where the stream's velocity is higher than the average velocity for the whole depth of the stream. Multiplying the surface velocity by 0.8 gives you a more accurate result for the average velocity of the whole stream.)

Resources
1 Visuals 1 and 2.
2 DATA FILE.
3 The Method and Worked Example.
4 It is quite easy to measure the discharge of streams and small rivers. A small current flowmeter (Visual 1) can be used, but it is possible to obtain accurate figures without expensive equipment. This is all you will need:

tape measure   metre ruler   orange
clipboard   two poles   wellington boots
pen   paper   watch with a second hand

1 A small current flowmeter

WORKED EXAMPLE
The following calculations are based on measurements taken on the Afon Llia in July 1986 at point A on visual 2.

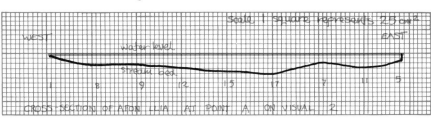

Scale 1 square represents 25 cm²

CROSS SECTION OF AFON LLIA AT POINT A ON VISUAL 2

(A) Fieldwork Measurements.
Width of channel (cm) 390

Distance from west bank (cm)	0	50	100	150	200	250	300	350	390
Depth of water	1	8	9	12	15	17	7	11	5

Recorded times for orange over 10 metre distance (in seconds)

Run:	1	2	3	4	5	6	7	8	9	10	total: 460 seconds
Time:	81	50	27	25	42	38	29	56	42	70	

Average time 46 seconds.

(B) Discharge Calculations
The stream cross-section is plotted on graph paper (as above).
Cross-section area: 160 squares × 25 square cm = 4000 square cm = 4000/10,000
= 0.4 Square m

Velocity in m per second = 10/46 = 0.217 m per second.
Discharge = 0.217 × 0.4 = 0.087 cumecs
Average discharge = 0.087 × 0.8 = 0.07 cumecs

The average discharge of the Afon Llia at Point A does not sound much, but in fact it works out at about six million litres of water a day. This is enough to supply the needs of 30,000 people!
(1000 litres of water takes up one cubic metre)

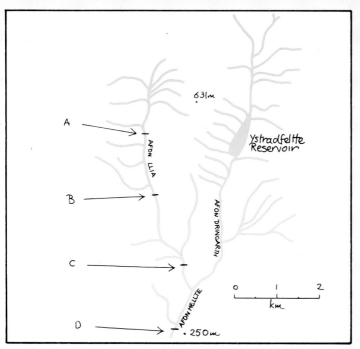

2 Survey points on the Afon Llia and Afon Mellte

FIELDWORK MEASUREMENTS ON THE AFON LLIA

Date 22 July 1986
Locations See Visual 2

POINT B

Width of channel 380 cm

Distance from west bank (cm)	0	50	100	150	200	250	300	350	380
Depth of water (cm)	24	31	34	34	36	33	37	34	24

Recorded times for orange over 10 m distance (seconds)

Run	1	2	3	4	5	6	7	8	9	10
Time	98	90	92	84	102	92	91	97	82	92

POINT C

Width of channel 480 cm

Distance from west bank (cm)	0	50	100	150	200	250	300	350	400	450	480
Depth of water (cm)	11	12	12	18	17	19	20	23	26	23	15

Recorded times for orange over 10 m distance (seconds)

Run	1	2	3	4	5	6	7	8	9	10
Time	55	79	67	68	72	56	77	71	66	59

POINT D

Width of channel 600 cm

Distance from west bank (cm)	0	50	100	150	200	250	300	350	400	450	500	550	600
Depth of water (cm)	5	10	5	12	21	18	15	15	10	4	3	3	5

Recorded times for orange over 10 m distance (seconds)

Run	1	2	3	4	5	6	7	8	9	10
Time	14	12	18	17	21	14	13	15	14	12

Work Programme A

1 Measurements were made at three further points on the Afon Llia (Visual 2). Study the measurements in the DATA FILE carefully. Calculate the discharge at the three points, by following the six instructions listed under Discharge Calculations.

2 At which point was the discharge greatest? Why was it greatest here?

3 The measurements were recorded during July. How do you think the measurements might differ if they were recorded during:
a) September   b) February?

4 a) Why were ten timed runs of the orange needed?

b) Why was it important to drop the orange at different points across the stream?

c) Why was it necessary to multiply the discharge figure by 0.8?

Work Programme B

Now choose your own section of a river and calculate the discharge. Try calculating the discharge several times over the period of a year. You will gain a useful insight into the changing nature of a river's discharge.

1 Lynmouth before the flood of 16 August 1952

WALL OF WATER BRINGS DEATH TO DEVON VILLAGE
Flooding of the River Lyn drowns 34 people.

This is an account of a flood on the River Lyn in North Devon which happened on 16 August 1952:

Down these gorges on that terrible night pounded millions of tonnes of flood water. In dry summer weather the rivers have a depth of a few centimetres; now, at times, a solid wall of water nearly 15 m high raced down to the sea at 30 km per hour. Such a torrent is irresistible to everything except the heaviest and most solidly based objects. The water gouged out huge rocks and boulders – some weighing 15 tonnes – and carried them to the shore. Telegraph poles and motor cars followed. Trees, felled by earlier gales, and others washed out by the roots, were swept into the sea. The next morning, half a mile out to sea, hundreds of trees, presumably weighted down by rocks and soil entangled in their enormous roots, had their upper branches showing above the waves – a fantastic sea forest of stunted trees.

The flood waters dug deep into the earth. Road surfaces were scoured away, and the soft earth of the verges was gouged as by a giant excavator, some gullies being 7 m deep – right down to bare rock. The Lynmouth sewerage system and water mains were wrecked. A vivid illustration of this gouging effect occurred at a Lynmouth garage. Here petrol tanks were scoured from their foundations and swept away without trace.

When dawn broke the scene on the shore was fantastic. It was littered with the debris of scores of wrecked homes and buildings; smashed cars; telegraph poles; tree trunks, branches and complete trees; the smashed and mangled remains of the undergrowth from the surrounding countryside; some 200 000 cubic metres of silt, mud, gravel and stones, in some places massed 8 m high; some 40 000 tonnes of rocks and boulders; iron girders and bridges; broken masonry; and the bodies of animals, birds, fish – and people.

(Adapted from *The Elements Rage* by F.W. Lane)

2 Damage following the Lynmouth flood

The flood killed 34 people. It destroyed 90 homes and swept 130 cars out to sea. The total damage cost £9 million (£110 million at 1987 prices). What caused such a disaster? The answer lies in a combination of the weather and the landscape of the area.

As Visual 3 shows, the East and West Lyn are short rivers which flow from Exmoor northwards to the Bristol Channel. They join on the coast, at Lynmouth, and flow in steep, narrow valleys called gorges.

The period before the flood had been wet. It had rained for 12 out of the previous 14 days. The ground was waterlogged. No more rain could soak into the thin soils which covered the hard, impermeable sandstone and slate rocks of Exmoor. On the day of the flood it rained extraordinarily hard. Normal steady rain for 24 hours measures about 25 mm in a rain gauge. At Lynmouth 230 mm of rain fell on 15 August. This is over a quarter of a million tonnes of water per square kilometre. Higher rainfall figures have been recorded only four times in Britain in the past 100 years.

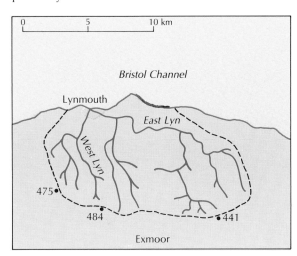

3 The drainage basin of the East and West Lyn rivers

1 *Compare the two photographs (Visuals 1 and 2). Give three pieces of evidence for the erosive power of the floodwater.*

2 *Working with your neighbour, first discuss and then write down how each of these factors helped to make the Lyn flood such a serious event:*

a) *The weather conditions.*

b) *The ground conditions and local geology.*

c) *The shape of the valley at Lynmouth.*

d) *The long profile of the two rivers.*

e) *The pattern of the rivers in the river basin.*

Use as much information as you can from the text, photographs and river basin map.

3 *If the circumstances had been different, the flood may have been different. Do you think that the flood would have been more or less serious if things had been different in each of the following ways. Give the full reasons for your answer in each case:*

a) *The shape of the valley at Lynmouth had been wider and less steep-sided.*

b) *300 mm of rain had fallen, but this was spread evenly over three days.*

c) *The rocks of Exmoor had been permeable.*

4 a) *Look up the area of Exmoor and the River Lyn in your atlas. The Lyn may not be marked, but you should be able to locate it from the coastal landmarks named in Visual 3.*

b) *On the same map locate the River Exe and its upper tributaries.*

c) *The upper part of the Exe also flows over Exmoor and would have experienced similar rainfall conditions as the Lyn on 16 August 1952. The flooding in the Exe valley was, however, not nearly as serious as in the Lyn valley. Using the atlas (and any other information on these pages) suggest as many reasons as you can to explain this.*

1 A push-tow barge on the River Rhône

2 Port Edouard Herriot

Visual 1 shows a modern push-tow barge travelling down a river in southern France. The river is the Rhône. Until recently the Rhône was a very difficult river to navigate because:

◦ The summer drought often reduced the depth of water to less than a metre.
◦ In the autumn and winter there were often serious floods due to torrential storms. The source of the Rhône is in the Swiss Alps. The melting of snow in the spring caused more floods.
◦ The current of the Rhône was always rapid and dangerous for shipping.

Now barge trains of up to 5000 tonnes can navigate the Rhône because of a massive scheme to develop the river. The scheme is a *multipurpose project*. In addition to improving navigation it has:

◦ Prevented flooding.
◦ Generated hydroelectricity.
◦ Encouraged industrial development.
◦ Extended the area of irrigated agriculture.

Twelve hydroelectric power stations have been built along the Rhône (Visual 3). They generate 20% of France's hydroelectricity. Loop canals (Visual 3, inset) have been built to divert part of the flow of the Rhône to the barrages containing the hydroelectric turbines. Locks have been built at the barrages. These have improved navigation by by-passing the most difficult sections of the river. Nine industrial estates have been built beside the Rhône (Visual 3). There are oil refineries, petrochemical plants, flour mills, cement works, metalworking and engineering factories. They all take advantage of the waterway's cheap transport of bulk raw materials.

Irrigation canals have been built at most of the hydroelectric power station sites. They have allowed the introduction of new crops into the Rhône valley. Fruit and vegetables have replaced the traditional wheat, olives and vines. Crops such as apples, peaches and tomatoes can earn up to five times as much as vines per hectare. Over 50 000 hectares are now irrigated. The barrages have also protected over 60 000 hectares of land from flooding.

1 a) *Using your atlas, draw a map showing the location of the River Rhône in France and Switzerland.*

  b) *Also mark on your map:*
    i) *The mountains where the river rises.*
    ii) *The countries and major cities through which the river flows.*
    iii) *The sea into which the river flows.*

2 a) *What problems did the River Rhône pose for navigation?*

  b) *How have these problems been overcome?*

3 *Study Visuals 2 and 3.*

  a) *Describe the scene in the photograph.*

  b) *Explain how the scheme allows the river to be used for both shipping and hydroelectric power.*

4 *How have the changes in the River Rhône affected industry and farming in the region?*

5 *The River Rhône scheme sounds a great success. Can you think of some people who might have regretted the changes? What might be their reasons?*

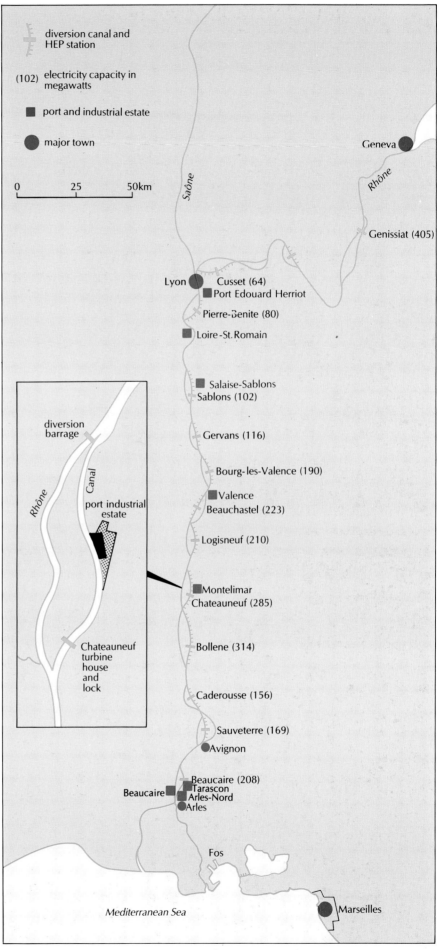

3 Power stations and industry along the River Rhône

ASSIGNMENT THREE
The Thames Flood Barrier

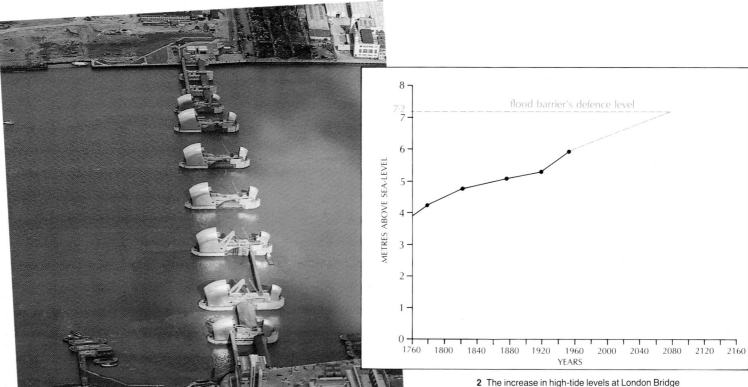

1 The Thames Flood Barrier

2 The increase in high-tide levels at London Bridge

London is slowly sinking! Why? There are two causes:

° The city is slowly settling into its bed of clay.

° Over the centuries, Britain itself is tilting. Scotland and the North West are rising, while the South East is gradually dipping downwards at the rate of about 2 cm every decade. This tilting is probably due to the Ice Age. During the Ice Age, deep ice sheets covered northern Britain and caused it to sink, while southern Britain rose. When the ice melted the situation was reversed. The north started to rise and the south to sink. The current tilting is simply the recovery, or rebound, 10 000 years after the ice finally melted.

As London sinks, the level of the River Thames seems to rise (Visual 2). London has been flooded many times in the past; the last major flood happened in 1928, when 14 people drowned. Conditions are most dangerous when a storm surge occurs (see page 54). To save London, a huge flood barrier has been built across the River Thames at Woolwich. This barrier will be effective until the year 2160; after that date a new barrier will have to be built further downriver. The map in Visual 3 shows places in danger of flooding before the building of the dam.

Your Assignment

You are working for the Thames Water Authority, in the Press and Public Relations Office. You have to:

° Prepare educational information for use in London schools.

Resources

1 Data provided in Visuals 1–3.

2 Details of a storm surge from page 54.

3 A large sheet of paper for your newspaper front page.

4 A tape recorder.

Work Programme

1 Imagine that the Thames Flood Barrier has not been built. Prepare and present the front page of a daily newspaper, describing the disastrous effects of serious floods in London. Do not forget to include illustrations with your article.

2 Using a tape recorder, present a radio programme on the flood disaster and its effects. Include interviews with survivors.

3 Design and produce a four-sided pamphlet on the Thames Flood Barrier, explaining the need for the Barrier and details of the Barrier itself. You should include illustrations.

3 The map (above right) shows the flood area before the Thames Barrier was built. The diagram below shows how the Thames Flood Barrier works

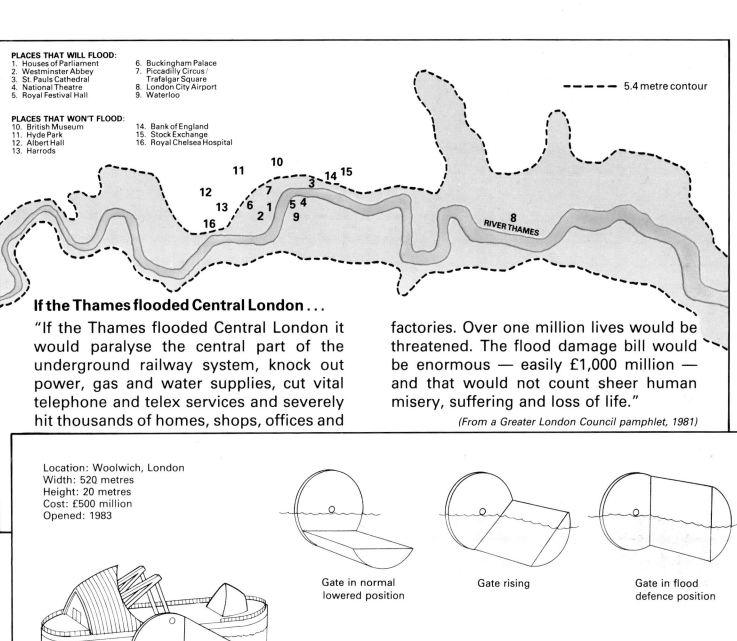

PLACES THAT WILL FLOOD:
1. Houses of Parliament
2. Westminster Abbey
3. St. Pauls Cathedral
4. National Theatre
5. Royal Festival Hall
6. Buckingham Palace
7. Piccadilly Circus / Trafalgar Square
8. London City Airport
9. Waterloo

PLACES THAT WON'T FLOOD:
10. British Museum
11. Hyde Park
12. Albert Hall
13. Harrods
14. Bank of England
15. Stock Exchange
16. Royal Chelsea Hospital

- - - - - 5.4 metre contour

RIVER THAMES

If the Thames flooded Central London . . .

"If the Thames flooded Central London it would paralyse the central part of the underground railway system, knock out power, gas and water supplies, cut vital telephone and telex services and severely hit thousands of homes, shops, offices and factories. Over one million lives would be threatened. The flood damage bill would be enormous — easily £1,000 million — and that would not count sheer human misery, suffering and loss of life."

(From a Greater London Council pamphlet, 1981)

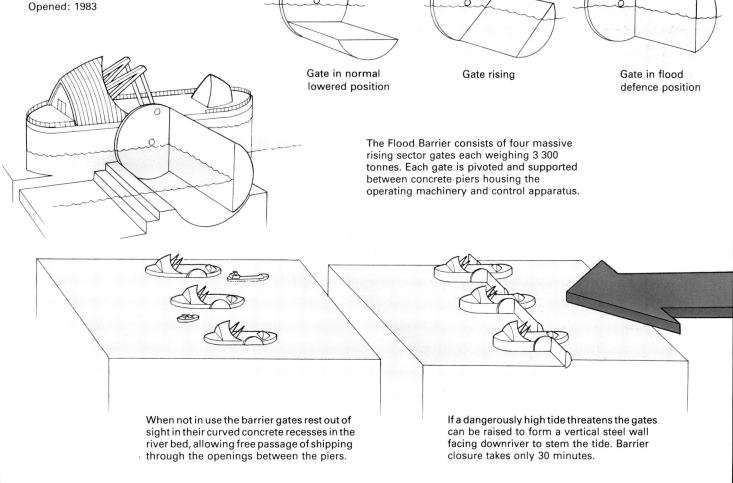

Location: Woolwich, London
Width: 520 metres
Height: 20 metres
Cost: £500 million
Opened: 1983

Gate in normal lowered position

Gate rising

Gate in flood defence position

The Flood Barrier consists of four massive rising sector gates each weighing 3 300 tonnes. Each gate is pivoted and supported between concrete piers housing the operating machinery and control apparatus.

When not in use the barrier gates rest out of sight in their curved concrete recesses in the river bed, allowing free passage of shipping through the openings between the piers.

If a dangerously high tide threatens the gates can be raised to form a vertical steel wall facing downriver to stem the tide. Barrier closure takes only 30 minutes.

1 Read the newspaper cutting carefully. In your atlas, find the places mentioned and answer the following questions:

a) What was the height of the waves? What caused the waves to be so large?

b) What were the wind speed and direction?

c) How do you think that the wind speed and direction affected the storm?

d) What effects did the storm have on both the physical and human landscape?

e) Make a list of all the ways in which the sea can alter the coastline. Compare your list with your neighbour's and produce a joint list.

From time to time we are reminded of the power and threat of the sea by newspaper stories. Storms can change even the most peaceful stretch of coast into a place of danger. Waves crash relentlessly on to the coast, battering the beaches and cliffs, hurling sand and pebbles onshore.

STORM LASHES SOUTH COAST : FOUR DIE

Storm waves over five metres high lashed the coast of Devon yesterday. South westerly winds of up to 150 kilometres per hour forced ships to seek shelter and battered coastal resorts. Two people were drowned when their yacht capsized off Salcombe. Two others are missing presumed dead after being swept away from the seafront at Sidmouth.

Considerable damage was caused to buildings and sea defences. Cliff falls at Lyme Regis forced two families to leave their homes and undermined the coastal road.

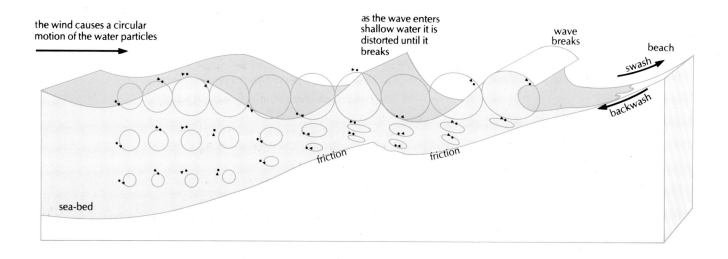

the wind causes a circular motion of the water particles

as the wave enters shallow water it is distorted until it breaks

wave breaks

beach

swash

backwash

friction

friction

sea-bed

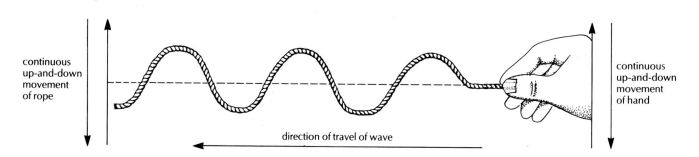

continuous up-and-down movement of rope

continuous up-and-down movement of hand

direction of travel of wave

2 Wave motion, as demonstrated by a rope

Waves

Waves are caused by the wind. The friction of the wind on the water creates ripples, which will grow into waves if the wind continues to blow. Within a wave each water particle moves in a circle and returns to its starting point (Visual 1). The water itself does not move forward, only the surge of energy. The same effect can be demonstrated by using a rope tied to a fixed object. Just a flick of the wrist can make the rope jump as a wave passes through the whole length of the rope. After the wave has passed, the rope returns to its original position. Only the wave travels forward, neither the rope nor the sea.

When the wave reaches shallow water, however, it is slowed by friction between the sea and the sea-bed. As the water begins to 'pile up', the wave loses its regular pattern. Soon the wave breaks. Now the water actually moves forward. Water moves up the beach as the swash and drains back again as the backwash.

The height and strength of the wave is affected by the distance over which the wave has been formed (the fetch of the wave). Visual 3 shows the different fetches affecting the coast of Dorset. A southerly wind will not produce large waves because the fetch is less than 150 km. However, a southwesterly wind may produce very large waves because its fetch may be as much as 7000 km.

Coastal Erosion

The sea erodes a cliff in five main ways:

- Waves can carry away loose or weakened rock.
- Waves can compress air into the joints of coastal rocks. The compressed air explodes as the waves retreat. Storm waves may exert pressure up to 30 tonnes per square metre in this way, enough to loosen the strongest rock.
- Waves hurl rock fragments against the cliff face, wearing away the cliff. This process is called corrasion.
- The rock fragments washing around on the beach are smashed together by the waves and further broken up. This process is called attrition.
- The process of solution occurs on limestone and chalk coasts. The sea water dissolves the calcium carbonate in these rocks and seriously weakens them.

These five processes are important only at the base of the cliff. Wind, rain and frost also attack the rest of the cliff, causing landslips and rockfalls.

2 a) *What causes a wave?*

   b) *Why does a wave break?*

3 a) *What is the fetch of a wave?*

   b) *Using an atlas to help you, calculate the length of fetch for waves approaching south Devon from the following directions:*
   i) south   ii) south east   iii) south west.
   From which direction is the fetch greatest?

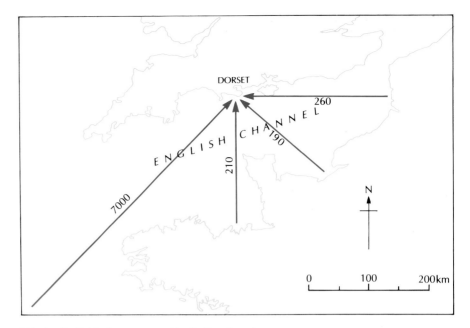

3 The length of fetch of waves approaching the Dorset coast

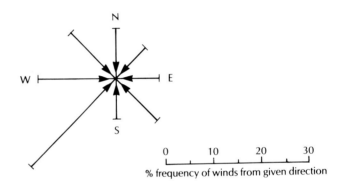

4 Frequency of winds on the Dorset coast

4 *Visual 4 shows for how much of the time the wind blows in a particular direction on the Dorset coast.*

   a) *Which is the most common, or prevailing, wind direction?*

   b) *Bearing in mind the length of fetch affecting the Dorset coast, what effect will the prevailing wind have upon the wave energy?*

5 *'Waves are a forward movement of energy, not water.' Explain what this means.*

5 A surfer rides the breaking wave

41

HANDFAST POINT

OLD HARRY

D

C

A

B

1 The Foreland, Dorset

Erosional Landforms

Visual 1 shows the Foreland, a chalk headland near Swanage in Dorset. At one time the two islands were joined to the mainland. Erosion has created several landforms here. At A is a cave formed by the widening of a joint in the chalk. At B is an arch where a cave has been eroded right through the headland. In the past there were arches at C and D. These were widened by erosion, until the roofs of the arches collapsed creating the two stacks, Old Harry and Handfast Point. The arch at B marks the beginning of the division of Handfast Point into two separate stacks. The sequence of erosion is shown opposite.

1 *What type of rock forms the headland in the photograph?*

2 *What is the evidence that some parts of the rock are more resistant to erosion than other parts?*

3 *What evidence is there that the sea is actively eroding the headland?*

4 *Was the photograph taken at high or low tide? What is the photographic evidence for your answer?*

THE EROSION OF A HEADLAND

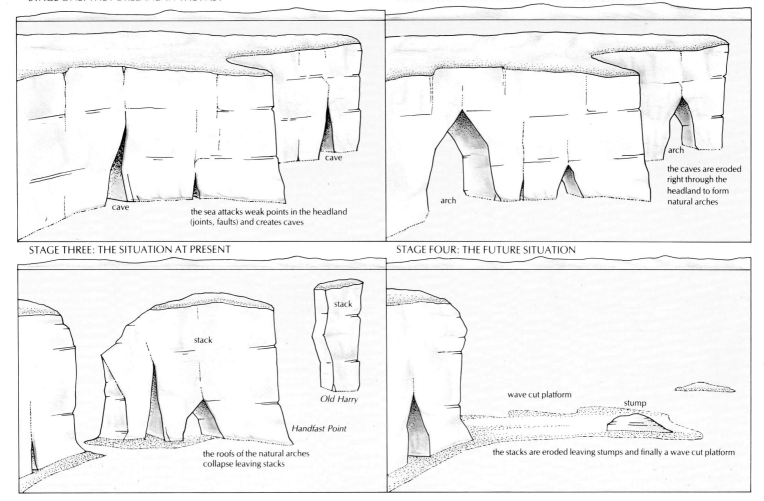

STAGE ONE: THE FORELAND IN THE PAST

cave

cave

the sea attacks weak points in the headland
(joints, faults) and creates caves

STAGE TWO: THE SITUATION IN THE MORE RECENT PAST

arch

arch

the caves are eroded
right through the
headland to form
natural arches

STAGE THREE: THE SITUATION AT PRESENT

stack

stack

Old Harry

Handfast Point

the roofs of the natural arches
collapse leaving stacks

STAGE FOUR: THE FUTURE SITUATION

wave cut platform

stump

the stacks are eroded leaving stumps and finally a wave cut platform

The Foreland is part of a series of bays and headlands along the coast from Durlston Head to South Haven Point (Visual 2). The shape of the coast results from the pattern of rock types. Bays have been formed where weaker rocks outcrop at the coast, headlands where there are more resistant rocks. This uneven, or indented, coastline is called a transverse coast. Where the rocks outcrop parallel to the coast, a longitudinal coastline is formed.

The processes of coastal erosion operate at different rates depending upon a number of factors. These include the wave fetch, the resistance and structure of the rock and the pattern of rock types. People also have a great effect upon the rate of erosion, as we shall see in the next spread.

5 *The box above shows the different stages in the erosion of a headland. Draw your own simple diagrams of what is happening at each stage. Add notes to your diagrams, naming the landforms and explaining how they are formed.*

6 *Suggest how each of these factors can affect the rate at which a stretch of coastline is eroded:*

   a) *The resistance of the rocks.*

   b) *The structure of the rocks.*

   c) *The pattern of rock types.*

   d) *The actions of people.*

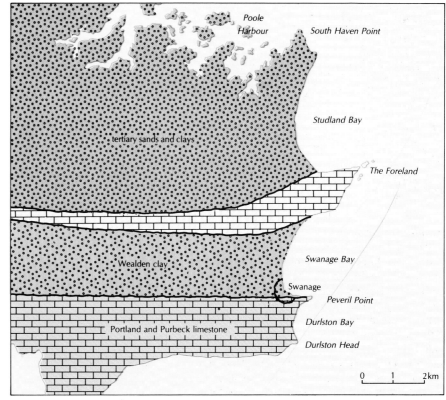

Poole Harbour

South Haven Point

Studland Bay

The Foreland

tertiary sands and clays

Swanage Bay

Wealden clay

Swanage

Peveril Point

Durlston Bay

Portland and Purbeck limestone

Durlston Head

0   1   2km

2 An example of a transverse coast

ASSIGNMENT FOUR

The Dorset Coast Around Lulworth Cove

1 The rounded shores of Lulworth Cove

2 The deep cleft of Stair Hole

The south Dorset coast features some of the most attractive coastal scenery in England and the Dorset Coast Path is one of the most heavily used coastal footpaths. Within a short distance, lie three spectacular landforms. Visual 1 shows Lulworth Cove, an almost circular bay backed by steep and impressive cliffs. Half a kilometre west of the cove is Stair Hole (Visual 2), a deep gash in the cliffs. One kilometre further west lies Durdle Door (Visual 3), a remarkable archway. Visual 4 shows the location of these landforms and the geology of the area.

Your Assignment

You work for the British Tourist Authority in the Publicity Department. There are three people in your section of the Department. Your assignment is based on the letter which you have received from Dorset County Council.

Resources

1 Data provided in the letter from Dorset County Council.

2 Data provided by Visuals 1–4.

3 A map of the coast in your atlas.

4 An Ordnance Survey map of the Lulworth area (OS 1:50 000 Sheet 194).

Greetings from Durdle Door

3 Durdle Door: a natural arch

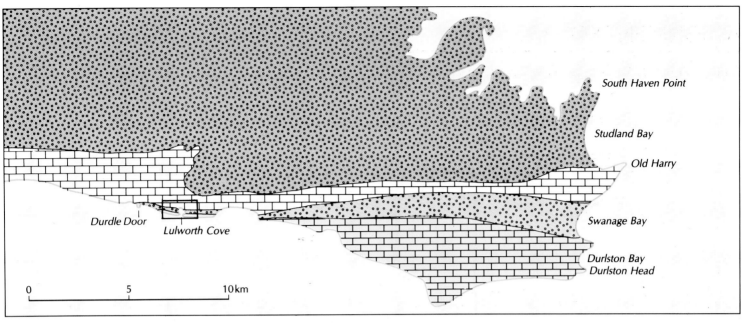

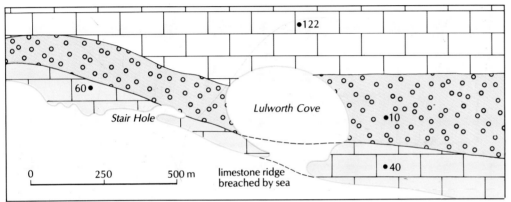

4 The geology of the Dorset coast

Legend:
- sands and clays (Reading beds, Bagshot sands)
- chalk
- sand and clays (Wealden clay, greensand)
- limestone (Portland and Purbeck beds)
- ● height above sea-level (metres)

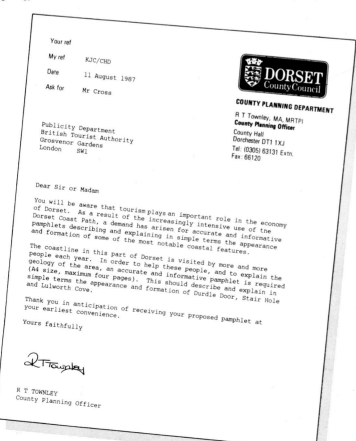

Work Programme

Work in groups of three.

1. a) Read the letter from Dorset County Council.
   b) Discuss the letter and make sure that you understand it.

2. Use the information given here to design a series of visuals to show the following:
   a) A sketch map of Britain highlighting the location of the south Dorset coast.
   b) Labelled sketch maps of Lulworth Cove, Stair Hole and Durdle Door.
   c) A labelled sketch of Durdle Door.

3. Prepare a written summary of the processes which have formed the three landforms.

4. Each group member should design a possible format for the information pamphlet. When the three designs are complete, study them as a group. Discuss their good and bad points and decide upon a final design.

5. Put your pamphlet together and hand it in.

1 The groyne at Hengistbury Head

On the Dorset coast, east of Bournemouth, is a headland of resistant sandstone called Hengistbury Head. A large concrete breakwater, or *groyne*, has been built there (Visual 1).

1 Study Visual 1 carefully. It is taken from the cliff top looking out to sea across Hengistbury Head groyne.

a) Make a sketch of the main features in the photograph.

b) Was the photograph taken at a high or low state of the tide?

c) On which side of the groyne is the beach wider?

d) On which side of the groyne is the water deeper?

e) What is happening at point A?

f) Describe the appearance of the area enclosed by the fence at B.

2 Try to explain the different appearance of the beach on each side of the groyne.

The groyne was built in 1938. Before that time there was a narrow beach along the full length of the headland. It is clear that the groyne has caused a large build up of sand to the west of the groyne, and a reduction of sand to the east. At high tide there is no beach at all east of the groyne; whilst to the west, sand dunes have developed. This could not have happened unless there was a movement of beach material along the coast, from west to east, at Hengistbury Head. This movement is called longshore drift. Visual 2 shows the process of this.

Depositional Landforms

Longshore drift provides the link between erosion and deposition along the coast. Material eroded from the cliff at one place will be transported along the coast and deposited elsewhere (Visual 3).

Several landforms result from this deposition. East of the groyne at Hengistbury Head the coastline turns northwards. A narrow section of lowland extends across the mouth of Christchurch Harbour. This narrow land is a *spit*. Mudeford Spit has been formed where the coastline abruptly changes direction. Longshore drift has continued in a northerly direction, depositing material to form the spit. Notice that *salt marsh* has developed in the sheltered water behind the spit.

Before the construction of the groyne, Mudeford Spit was much longer and broader than it is today. The supply of material by longshore drift has been much reduced by the Hengistbury Head groyne. Groynes have now had to be built on the spit itself to prevent the spit from being destroyed.

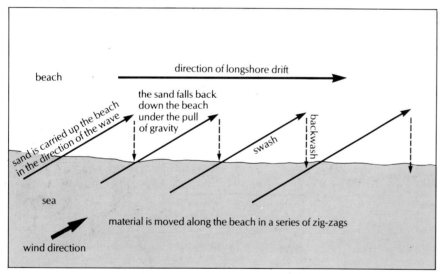

2 The process of longshore drift

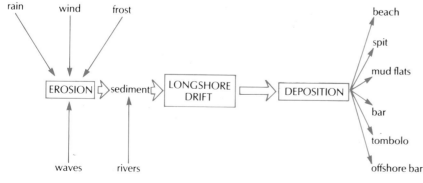

3 Flow diagram showing the coastal system

The construction of the groyne has changed the balance of the coastal processes at Hengistbury Head. The beach west of the groyne has grown and the cliffs there are no longer reached by the sea. To the east, the beach and spit have been greatly reduced, as longshore drift has been cut off. The groyne may also have affected Christchurch Bay to the east.

Coastal Processes in Christchurch Bay

Since the 1930s, rapid coastal erosion has occurred in Christchurch Bay, most notably at Barton on Sea. The cliffs at Barton are 30 m high, but are formed in relatively weak sands and clays (Visual 5). The foot of the cliff is attacked by the sea and the cliff face is prone to slumping and rotational slip. Rainwater drains through the permeable Barton sands. It emerges as springs at the level of the water table, above the impermeable Barton clay. The water carries eroded material with it, thus undermining the cliff and causing collapse of the upper cliff. This has brought the cliff top dangerously near to several buildings.

A massive engineering scheme was carried out to protect the cliffs, at a cost of over £6 million. A sea wall and groynes were built at the foot of the cliff and sheet steel was driven into the cliff face. Despite this, the cliff still collapsed following heavy rain in 1975.

Engineers had tried to prevent the natural processes of erosion – and failed. One reason was that longshore drift was unable to build up enough beach material to protect the cliff foot. The longshore drift had probably been lessened due to the groyne at Hengistbury, 7 km to the west of Barton. Barton also faces the full force of the southwesterly gales.

Since 1975 the scheme has been renewed with the addition of thousands of limestone boulders along the cliff foot and a complex drainage system through the cliff face. Strong *promontories* have been built into the sea and an artificial beach has been made. Will this save Barton? Only time will tell.

3 a) *Draw your own diagrams to explain the process of longshore drift.*

   b) *How could you prove that longshore drift was happening on a stretch of coastline? What evidence could you collect?*

4 *Draw your own diagrams to explain how the following landforms are formed:*

   a) *spit   b) bar   c) tombolo.*

5 a) *What is meant by the 'balance of coastal processes'?*

   b) *How has the groyne at Hengistbury Head upset the natural balance of coastal processes?*

6 a) *Describe the coastal defence engineering scheme at Barton on Sea.*

   b) *How successful do you think the scheme has been?*

   c) *What else would you need to know to judge the long-term success of the scheme?*

7 *Working with your neighbour:*

   a) *Make a plan for measures to reduce further erosion at Barton.*

   b) *Draw up your plan as a report, including suitable maps and diagrams.*

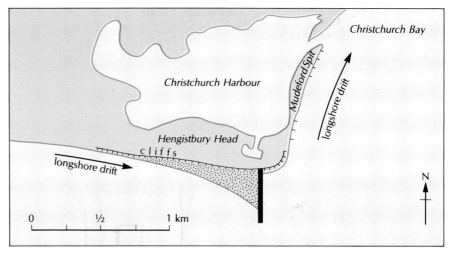

4 Hengistbury Head and Mudeford Spit

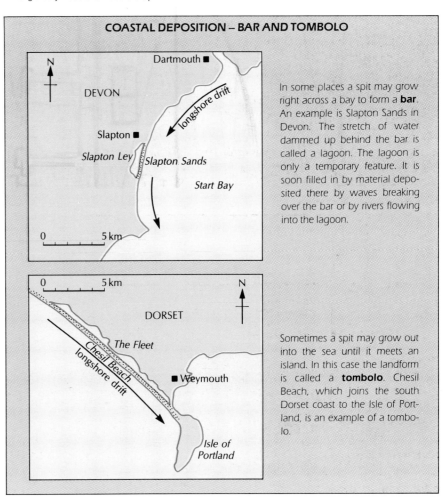

COASTAL DEPOSITION – BAR AND TOMBOLO

In some places a spit may grow right across a bay to form a **bar**. An example is Slapton Sands in Devon. The stretch of water dammed up behind the bar is called a lagoon. The lagoon is only a temporary feature. It is soon filled in by material deposited there by waves breaking over the bar or by rivers flowing into the lagoon.

Sometimes a spit may grow out into the sea until it meets an island. In this case the landform is called a **tombolo**. Chesil Beach, which joins the south Dorset coast to the Isle of Portland, is an example of a tombolo.

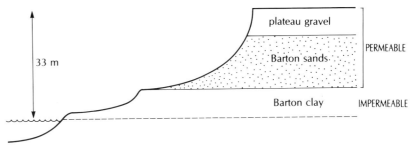

5 The Barton on Sea cliffs in cross-section

ASSIGNMENT FIVE
Save Kingsdown!

Kingsdown is a coastal resort in East Anglia. Coastal erosion has increased in recent years and several buildings are now dangerously close to the cliff top (Visual 1). Visual 2 shows a cross-section of the eroded cliff and Visual 3 shows the prevailing winds. The local council, East Norfolk District Council, has decided to invest in a major coastal protection scheme. The council has commissioned the London engineering company, Webber Engineers plc, to prepare plans for the protection of the coast.

Webber Engineers submitted two alternative plans, Option A and Option B. There has been strong opposition to the whole idea of a coastal protection scheme from two groups of people:

1 A group of people living inland in the East Norfolk District Council area. They call themselves the Inland Ratepayers Association (IRA). The IRA object to the schemes because of the high cost. Their chairperson, Michael Snelgrove, said: 'Why should the ratepayers pay for something that is of no benefit to the vast majority of us?'

2 The Council for the Preservation of Rural England (CPRE) and a number of scientific groups who object to the loss of the beach and cliffs beneath the civil engineering works. A spokesperson, Ms Anne Stamper, said: 'The coast at Kingsdown is an important habitat for plants and animals. This will be destroyed if the scheme goes ahead.'

A public enquiry has been called to consider the alternatives and decide whether the coastal protection scheme should go ahead or not.

Your Assignment
○ Prepare a report and a plan for protecting the coast at Kingsdown.
○ Take part in a public enquiry about the plan.
○ Come to a decision about the Kingsdown plan.

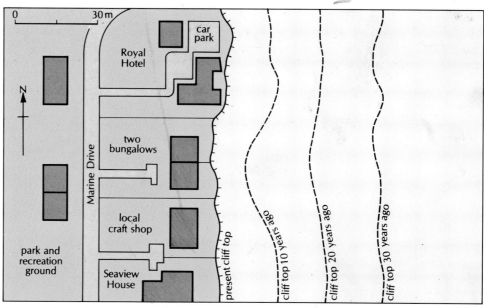

1 The retreat of the cliff top over 30 years

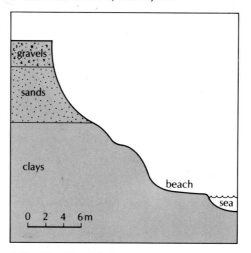

2 The cliffs at Kingsdown in cross-section

Resources
1 Visuals 1-3.
2 The submissions from the IRA and CPRE.
3 The table of costs of various engineering works.
4 The examples of coastal processes and coastal landforms studied on the previous pages.

Work Programme A

For the first part of your assignment you are going to work as a member of the Planning Team at Webber Engineers plc.

1 Form a small group and study all the information carefully.
2 Write a report on the situation at Kingsdown. Your report needs to:
   a) Explain the causes of the rapid coastal erosion.
   b) Predict what future effects the erosion will have on Kingsdown if nothing is done.
   c) Prepare two alternative plans for coastal protection schemes (Options A and B).
3 After completing your report, your team should prepare a 'Kingsdown Protection Plan':
   a) Include maps and diagrams if they will help others to understand.
   b) Explain your plans fully so that the East Norfolk District Council, and local people, will understand them.
4 Submit your plans to the whole class.
5 After class discussion, agree which group's plan should be presented to the East Norfolk District Council.

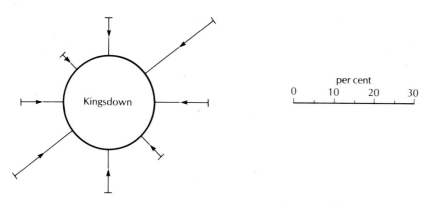

per cent

0   10   20   30

3 The percentage frequency of winds from a given direction

COSTS OF VARIOUS CIVIL ENGINEERING WORKS (per kilometre)		
	£	
Groynes	340 000	Reduce longshore drift, preserve beach
Sea walls	820 000	Protect base of cliff but lose beach
Groynes and sea walls	1 100 000	Protect base of cliff and preserve beach
Dumping of boulders on beach	20 000	Protect beach from wave attack
Drainage system	380 000	Reduce erosion of cliff face
Regular replacement of lost beach material	50 000 (per year)	Preserve beach without need to build groynes or sea walls; more effective if groynes also used.

SUBMISSION FROM THE COUNCIL FOR THE PRESERVATION OF RURAL ENGLAND

The cliffs and beach of the small seaside resort of Kingsdown represent a valuable part of our national heritage. This is one of the few remaining stretches of the East Anglian coast which has not been subjected to extensive commercial development. The resort of Kingsdown maintains the atmosphere and appeal of a time gone by. Coastal protection works would ruin the appearance and atmosphere of Kingsdown.

The cliffs at Kingsdown provide a geological site of national importance for the study of boulder clays from the Ice Age. In addition the cliffs in their natural state provide a valuable habitat for wildlife, both plant and animal. The geological site and the wildlife habitat would be destroyed by coastal protection works.

We recommend that no action be taken to protect the cliffs, that they be allowed to continue to erode naturally and that compensation be paid to the owners of the buildings which will be destroyed.

SUBMISSION FROM INLAND RATEPAYERS ASSOCIATION

The possible cost of the coast protection scheme is over a million pounds. The protection scheme will only directly help the owners of the six buildings threatened by cliff erosion. The total value of these six buildings has been estimated at £650,000. We maintain that it is a waste of ratepayers' money to protect the interests of such a small number of people. We also understand that the character of Kingsdown beach would be greatly altered by coastal defence works. We strongly object to this threatened loss of a valuable local amenity. We estimate that losses in income from lost tourist use of the beach, should the scheme go ahead, would exceed £100,000 per year.

We recommend that no protective action be taken. Compensation can be paid to the owners of the threatened buildings and considerable savings can thus be made.

Work Programme B

For the second part of your assignment, you are going to take the part of one of the interested parties at the public enquiry.

1 Join with others to form a small group who will be representing the views of one of these interested parties:

◦ The East Norfolk District Council.
◦ Webber Engineers plc.
◦ The Inland Ratepayers Association.
◦ The Council for the Protection of Rural England.
◦ The local residents of Kingsdown.
◦ The Kingsdown Chamber of Commerce and Tourism.

2 In your group discuss your views of the plan. Use the information given here to help prepare your case for the public enquiry.

3 Join the other groups to carry out the public enquiry. Each group should have the chance to make a short presentation of its case. After each presentation, allow the other groups to ask questions.

Work Programme C

A final decision will be made by an inspector who has been listening to the cases presented by each of the groups. Your job is now to take the role of the inspector.

1 Working on your own, think about what was said at the enquiry and come to a final decision. Here are just some of the decisions you could make:

a) The plan, as it now is, should be approved.
b) The plan should be changed in some ways.
c) The plan should be rejected.

2 Write a short report outlining your decision and giving your reasons for your decision.

1 Spurn Head

Visual 1 shows Spurn Head on the Humberside coast. Spurn Head is a spit which extends nearly half-way across the mouth of the Humber Estuary. The spit is 6 km long and forms a sweeping curve which continues the line of the coast. In places it is only a few metres wide. Spurn Head is owned by the Yorkshire Naturalists Trust and is an important wildlife reserve. Migrating birds shelter there. On the end of the spit there is a lighthouse and a lifeboat station.

The spit itself consists of sand and shingle with sand dunes colonized by marram grass and sea buckthorn. In the sheltered water to the west of the spit, fine river sediment has been deposited and some salt marshes have developed. The sand and shingle which make up the spit have been transported by the action of longshore drift from the north.

The erosion of the 60 km long coast between Flamborough Head and Spurn Head supplies the material for the spit. The cliffs along this coast are formed from sands and clays deposited by ice sheets. These sands and clays have little resistance to erosion. The coastline is receding by an average of 2 m per year, under the relentless attack of waves from the north and north east. Since Roman times this stretch of coastline has receded by up to 4 km.

Dozens of towns and villages have been lost during this process.

The coastal erosion is so rapid that Spurn Head has been repeatedly affected. Studies of old maps and charts show that the spit has been destroyed three times during the last six centuries. In the Middle Ages a port called Ravenser Odd developed on Spurn Head. Around AD 1360 Ravenser Odd was washed away. The spit formed again but was destroyed around 1608. Again the spit re-formed, only to be destroyed once more in 1849. The spit has re-formed a third time since 1849 and is currently growing by about 10 cm each year. Visual 3 shows the changing position of Spurn Head, as calculated partly from old maps.

Spurn Head seems to have a life of about 250 years before it is destroyed and re-formed. What causes this cycle of erosion and deposition? It is probable that the spit begins to grow out from the mainland as a result of the action of longshore drift. The spit gradually lengthens over a period of about 250 years until is is breached by waves and rapidly destroyed. Rapid erosion of the mainland alters the angle of contact of the spit with the mainland. The spit becomes starved of material and exposed to stronger wave attack. Then the spit begins to form again in a more westerly position.

1 Use the text and Visual 1 to describe Spurn Head.

2 a) Using your atlas, calculate the length of fetch of waves approaching the coast at Withernsea (north of Spurn Head) from the: north north east east south east.

b) Which section of the coast has retreated furthest? Do your calculations for length of fetch help to explain this?

3 It has been suggested that Spurn Head is built from material washed from the cliffs south of Flamborough Head. What evidence would you expect to find to support this?

4 Visual 4 is a cross-section through Spurn Head.

a) Why are the particle sizes at points A, B and C different?

b) Why is the eastern slope of the spit steeper than the western slope?

c) Why are the particle sizes at points A and D different?

5 The following plants are to be found on Spurn Head:

PLANT	HABITAT
sand sedge	sandy soils, sheltered dunes
willow	deep sandy soils
sea couch grass	tolerates salt water, exposed beaches
gorse	deep sandy soils
spartina	tolerates salt water, prefers shelter
sea buckthorn	sandy soils, sheltered dunes
heather	sandy soils
marram grass	freshly blown sand

a) Copy Visual 4.

b) On your cross-section, indicate where you would expect to find each plant growing. Underneath, make a brief note outlining the reasons for your choice.

6 Visuals 2 and 3 suggest that the position of Spurn Head is changing through time. Why do think this has happened? When would you expect Spurn Head to be breached again?

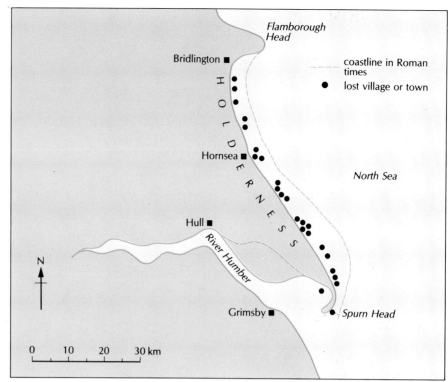

2 The erosion of the coast at Holderness

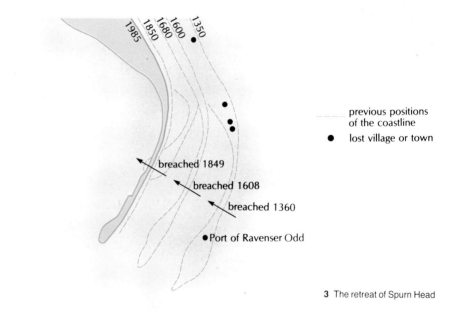

3 The retreat of Spurn Head

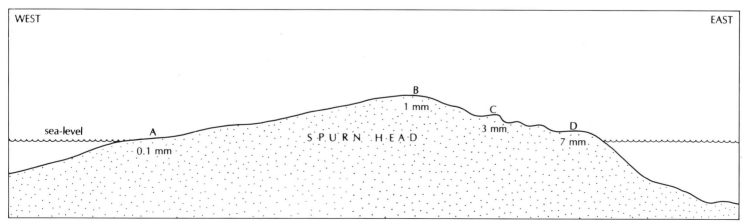

4 Spurn Head in cross-section

THE RHÔNE DELTA

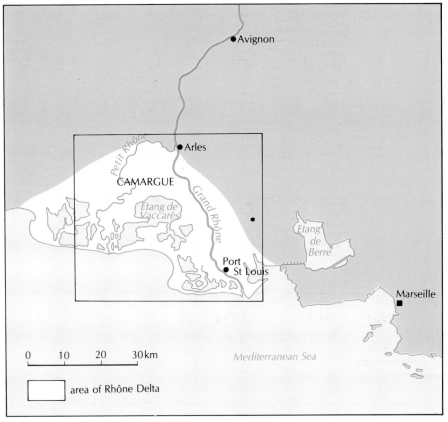

1 The river system of the Rhône Delta

2 Satellite photograph of the area shown boxed in Visual 1

Visual 1 shows the River Rhône entering the Mediterranean Sea. As it approaches the sea, the river divides into a number of channels called *distributaries*. The main distributaries are the Petit Rhône and the Grand Rhône. This triangle of flat, marshy land and lagoons is the *delta* of the River Rhône.

The Rhône is France's longest river. It transports a huge quantity of silt, sand and pebbles. Where the Rhône enters the Mediterranean, its speed is reduced and its load of sediment released. The delta has been built up over a long time. The box opposite shows the conditions which favour the formation of deltas. The vast amount of sediment and the low tidal range (only a few centimetres) have been the most important causes in the formation of the Rhône Delta. This delta is an example of an arcuate or fan-shaped delta. Two other types of delta are shown in the box opposite.

The area of the Rhône Delta is known as the Camargue. This remote area was once one of the most mysterious and romantic areas of France. The shape and form of the delta were constantly changing until people started to control the distributaries and sea in the 1800s. Dykes and sea walls were built and distributaries were re-routed. Salty lagoons and marshes now mark places where the distributaries once flowed.

Nine thousand people live in the Camargue and their main occupation is farming. Most of the soil is poor – only the alluvium in the north and along the distributaries is fertile. Vines, fruit, sunflowers and rice are grown with the aid of irrigation. Elsewhere the pasture land is grazed by cattle and horses. Camargue bulls are reared for bull fighting. The land is mainly farmed in vast estates and large areas are reserved for duck shooting and fishing. In the south east of the Camargue most of Europe's sea salt is produced. Sea water is trapped in large shallow basins and when the water evaporates it leaves the salt behind.

The remoteness of the Camargue, once a problem, has become an advantage. Remoteness is now sought by tourists. Over a million tourists visit the Camargue each year. They are attracted by the sunshine, sandy beaches and wildlife; by the image of wild bulls, white horses and cowboys. The Camargue is one of Europe's most important wildfowl reserves; herons, ducks, geese and, most famous of all, pink flamingoes live there. Tourists are catered for by hotels, guest houses, open air museums, pony trekking centres and other amenities. The Camargue was designated a Regional Nature Park in 1970.

Several steps have been taken to safeguard the area. At the heart of the park is a national nature reserve which the public cannot enter. Around this is a second zone where access is controlled, but tourism is permitted. A third peripheral zone covers the main access roads and the coast. This is open to the public without any restrictions, but there is control over traffic. Despite these measures, the character of the Camargue is threatened by the demands of intensive farming and tourism.

BIRD'S FOOT DELTA

Example: River Mississippi, USA

The river carries very large amounts of silt. The silt is deposited a long way out to sea along the edge of the channels.

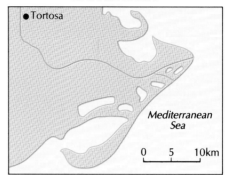

CUSPATE DELTA

Example: River Ebro, Spain

Cuspate means shaped like a tooth. Such a delta is formed when one major channel carries most of the silt down to the sea.

CONDITIONS FAVOURING THE FORMATION OF DELTAS

- Large amount of silt.
- More deposition than erosion.
- Shallow water off the river's mouth.
- Coastline sheltered from strong waves and currents.
- Small tidal range.
- Stable sea-level.

1 Explain why deltas form at the mouth of rivers such as the Rhône.

2 The Rhône Delta is no longer a constantly changing landform. Why not?

3 Make a list of how people use the Rhône Delta region today.

4 a) How has the development of tourism in the Camargue been controlled?

   b) Why was it necessary to put controls on the development of tourism in the Camargue?

5 Using an atlas, find the following rivers and say what type of delta they possess: Niger (Nigeria) Indus (Pakistan) Ganges (India/Bangladesh) Po (Italy) Orinoco (Venezuela).

6 a) Using an atlas to help you, draw a map of Egypt.

   b) Mark on your map the course of the River Nile and the Nile Delta.

   c) Using the map in your atlas which shows density of population in Africa, shade in the areas of Egypt which have over 100 people per square km.

   d) Describe the distribution of population revealed by your map and try to explain it.

7 Study the material in the box above and suggest why there are no major deltas on the coast of Britain.

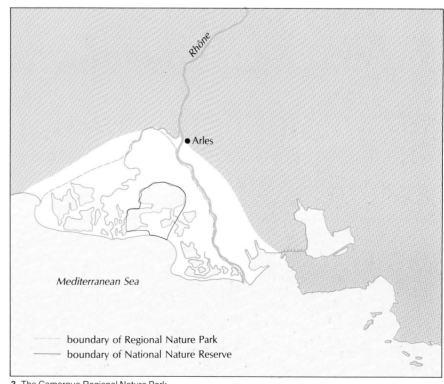

boundary of Regional Nature Park
boundary of National Nature Reserve

3 The Camargue Regional Nature Park

Visual 1 shows the weather situation on the night of 31 January 1953. A very deep depression moved southwards across the North Sea, causing a *storm surge*. Hurricane-force winds pushed water into the North Sea from the Atlantic Ocean. In addition, the very low atmospheric pressure caused the level of the sea to rise about 60 cm higher than normal. Water was piled up against the North Sea coasts by the storm. The sea-level was highest in the confined areas of estuaries. In the Thames estuary, the sea-level rose by over 3 m and swept across the low coastal areas. Canvey Island was submerged. Sixty people were drowned in eastern England, most of them in Canvey. This tragic event was the result of the storm surge combining with a high spring tide.

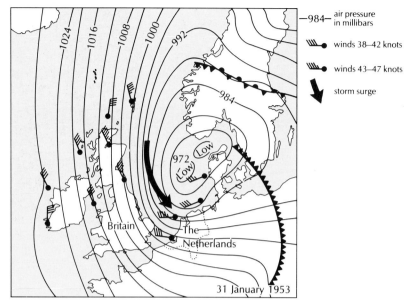

—984— air pressure in millibars

winds 38–42 knots

winds 43–47 knots

storm surge

1 The weather map on 31 January 1953

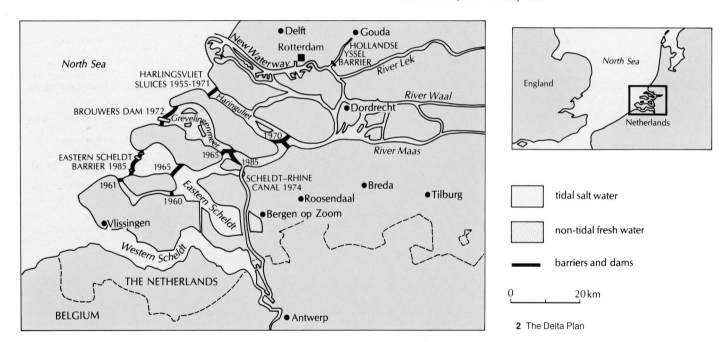

tidal salt water

non-tidal fresh water

barriers and dams

0   20 km

2 The Delta Plan

Whilst the 1953 storm surge had tragic results in England, this was overshadowed by the disaster which it caused in the Netherlands. Much of the Dutch coastal lands are very low-lying and have been reclaimed from the sea. In 1953 the sea broke through the dykes and sea walls: 150 000 hectares of land were flooded, over 10 000 houses were destroyed, 1850 people and 25 000 livestock were drowned, most of them in the delta of the Rivers Scheldt, Rhine and Maas.

The Dutch were determined that such a disaster should never happen again. A commission recommended the closure of four of the five sea channels in the delta by constructing four massive

dams and four smaller barriers. The fifth channel, the Western Scheldt, had to be kept open to allow ships to enter the Belgian port of Antwerp. To the north of the delta, the New Waterway was also to be kept open for the port of Rotterdam. This huge scheme was known as the Delta Plan (Visual 2).

1 *What caused the North Sea flood disaster of 1953?*

2 *How did the disaster affect: a) England*
   b) the Netherlands?

3 *Using Visual 2 to help you, describe the main features of the Delta Plan.*

The Delta Act was passed by the Dutch Parliament in 1958. The dams to be built under the Delta Plan would reduce the length of the Dutch coastline by over 700 km. Other dams had to be built further inland to give yet more control to movements of water. The storm surge barrier across the river Hollandse Yssel provides an example. Two large guillotine gates can be lowered to prevent flooding through the open mouth of the New Waterway.

The plan aimed to protect the region from flooding, but it had several other effects. As the 'Results of the Delta Plan' shows, the other effects of the plan were not all good. As construction proceeded, opposition increased from people worried by the loss of the coastal fisheries, oyster beds and the tidal mudflats. The delta was a very important wintering ground for wildfowl. By 1973, three of the large dams had been completed. Only the largest dam, that across the Eastern Scheldt, was unfinished. Five kilometres of the estuary mouth had already been dammed.

It was in 1973 that the government ordered a further study to discover whether the Eastern Scheldt could remain open to the sea. In 1976, Parliament approved the recommended change to the plan. The planned dam across the Eastern Scheldt was scrapped and replaced by a movable flood barrier. The barrier would allow the normal operation of the tides and would only be closed when flooding threatened. It is similar to the Thames flood barrier, but on a much larger scale. The Thames barrier is 500 m long; the Eastern Scheldt barrier is 3 km long. Whereas the Thames barrier has four movable gates, the Eastern Scheldt has 63!

Public attitudes to the Delta Plan have changed. Admiration for the technical achievement remains, but anxiety over the damage which the scheme could cause has become uppermost. The general view now is that compromise is needed between flood prevention and conservation. By deciding to construct a barrier rather than a dam, the cost of the Delta Plan was increased by £400 million. Completion was delayed until 1986, a period of eight years. However, the *ecology* of the Eastern Scheldt will be much less damaged by the barrier. The tidal mudflats, the wading birds, fish and oysters will continue to thrive and the people of the delta will still be safe from floodwaters of the North Sea.

4 Study the 'Results of the Delta Plan'. Divide the results of the Delta Plan into two lists, one showing those results which you think were welcome and those which you think were unwelcome.

5 a) Form a group of four people. Imagine you have been brought together in 1973 to discuss the future of the Eastern Scheldt.

   b) Each group member should take one of these roles:

   ◦ A planner from the Dutch Public Works Department (the Rijkswaterstaat), whose task is to complete the Eastern Scheldt defences as quickly and efficiently as possible.

   ◦ A representative of the Dutch government, whose task is to be aware of public opinion and to arrive at the most politically advantageous decision (bearing in mind the need to protect life and property and to save money).

3 The Eastern Scheldt storm surge barrier

RESULTS OF THE DELTA PLAN

At a cost of over £3000 million, the Delta Plan has protected over five million people's homes from flooding by the sea. Freshwater reservoirs have been created for drinking water and for the Delta's growing industrial demand. The reservoirs also provide sheltered water for recreation and the removal of the sea water has reduced the damage done by salt seeping on to farmland.

15000 hectares of land have been reclaimed for housing and industry. Road links have been improved via the dams and ferries have been replaced. A new non-tidal ship canal has been built to link the rivers Rhine and Scheldt.

Not all the results of the Delta Plan have been so good. Large areas of tidal mudflats have been lost, destroying the habitat of rare wading birds. Some valuable oyster and mussel beds have been lost. The replacement of sea by freshwater has meant the loss of some of the Netherland's richest inshore fishing grounds.

Tidal plant and animal communities have been replaced by freshwater communities. Nature reserves have been created to protect the new habitats.

   ◦ A representative of the oyster fishermen who work in the Eastern Scheldt estuary, and whose livelihood is threatened by the original dam proposal.

   ◦ A representative of a Dutch environmental group.

   You should prepare a detailed description of your own opinions concerning the original proposal for the construction of a dam across the Eastern Scheldt. You should have facts to support your case and should make proposals for the future development of the area.

   c) Hold a discussion presenting your cases in turn, starting with the planner. Discuss each case.

   d) The representative of the Dutch government should decide the best course to follow and justify her or his decision to the members of the group.

6 How and why was the Delta Plan modified after 1973?

ASSIGNMENT SIX

The Battle of Goodbury

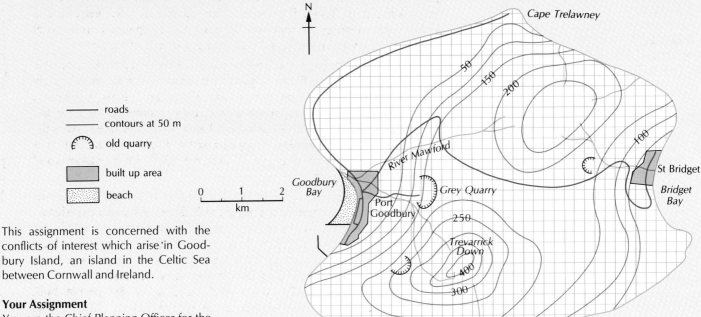

Legend:
- —— roads
- —— contours at 50 m
- ⌒ old quarry
- ▒ built up area
- ░ beach

0 1 2 km

This assignment is concerned with the conflicts of interest which arise in Goodbury Island, an island in the Celtic Sea between Cornwall and Ireland.

Your Assignment

You are the Chief Planning Officer for the island.

- Study the conflicts of interest which exist in the island.
- Suggest some solutions.
- Suggest how the island might develop in the future to avoid these conflicts.

Resources

1 DATA FILE.
2 Book extract.
3 Extracts from letters to newspapers.
4 Map of Goodbury Island.
5 Future Developments Simulation and cards A–I (pages 58 and 59).

Work Programme

Your job is to prepare a report with the following sections:

1 The Goodbury Scene
Describe what the island is like. (Before continuing your report you should complete the three rounds of the Future Developments Simulation.)

2 Conflicts of Interest
Identify the conflicts of interest which have existed in the past, which exist today, and which may arise in the future.

3 Goodbury's Future Development
Suggest what should be allowed and what should not be allowed to develop in the island. Try to avoid conflicts of interest.

FUTURE DEVELOPMENTS SIMULATION

WHAT TO DO

1 Copy the map of Goodbury Island.
2 Throw a die. Refer to the table below, Round One.
3 Study the appropriate Game Card and carry out the instructions.
4 Repeat for Rounds Two and Three.
5 Complete your report for handing in.

IF YOU THROW	ROUND ONE	ROUND TWO	ROUND THREE
⚁ or	Application to re-open Grey Quarry (see Card A)	Application to build a container terminal at Port Goodbury (see Card D)	Application to build a holiday village at St Bridget (see Card G)
⚃ or	Serious coastal erosion at Port Goodbury (see Card B)	Landslip at St Bridget (see Card E)	Serious flooding of River Mawford affects Port Goodbury (see Card H)
⚅ or	Application to build an airstrip for light aircraft (see Card C)	Application to build ten retirement homes (see Card F)	Application to build a crude oil terminal at Port Goodbury (see Card I)

GOODBURY ISLAND

POPULATION
2656 (1987 estimate)

MAIN SETTLEMENTS
Port Goodbury (1814 persons)
St Bridget (496 persons)

MAIN OCCUPATIONS (1981 census)
Goodbury Woollen Mill (34 employees)
Ace Electronics (22 employees)
Grey Quarry (66 employees)
Shops (43 employees)
Post Office (3 employees)
Public Houses, Cafés and Restaurants
    (33 employees)
Goodbury Bird Sanctuary (4 employees)
Garage (4 employees)
Port Work (5 employees)
Goodbury Island Ferry Company (12 employees)
Fishing (9 employees)
Farming (32 employees)
Teachers, Nurses, Police and Other Services
    (30 employees)

EXTRACT FROM *A GUIDE TO BRITAIN'S ISLANDS* BY ERNEST SAYERS (1985):

The passenger approaching Goodbury Island by boat from England will be struck by the steep granite cliffs rising sheer from the dark waters of the Celtic Sea. Low clouds often shroud the summit of Trevarrick Down. The scream of gulls, gannets and puffins reaches the boat over the noise of the engines. This is a vital sanctuary and breeding ground for many species of sea bird.

After rounding Cape Trelawney, Goodbury's softer side becomes apparent. Large fields of pasture lie inland, behind broad sandy beaches. Granite farm cottages face the Atlantic gales, strong and secure, almost an extension of the rocky granite outcrops further inland. Farming on the island is a harsh life and in recent years the number of farmers has dropped rapidly. Even from the boat it is possible to see the dead eyes of some cottages, with no windows and threadbare roofs.

The boat docks at the little harbour of Port Goodbury. The stone harbour walls were built during the 19th century when the island's granite trade was at its height. Now the trade has finally ended with the closure, in 1982, of the last quarry. Port Goodbury's once busy harbour now waits for the daily ferry boat – or an occasional coaster. Even the island's fishing fleet has dwindled to just a handful of inshore boats. Port Goodbury itself is a village of 1800 people, built of the granite which forms much of the island. Outside Port Goodbury and St Bridget there are no settlements of over 50 people – just the occasional hamlet hidden in the brooding landscape.

Goodbury Island gives the impression of a place which has seen better times. The world, no longer interested in its granite or sheep, now passes it by. As a result it is the perfect holiday retreat for the tourist who really wants to get away from it all.

29

Extract from letter to the Island's Newspaper "The Goodbury Globe" by local resident Michael St John Burrowes

YOUR LETTERS

during
e other
Parish
Central
march

Hon.
General
Council

Derek
y of
for

ohns,

ged.

t St.
ning
will

As summer approaches the people of Port Goodbury prepare themselves for another invasion of tourists. Noise, litter, congestion and crime accompany these unwelcome visitors. Even more of a threat to our way of life are those tourists who "fall in love" with the island and decide to buy a holiday home. This raises the prices of houses on Goodbury and makes it impossible for our children to afford houses on their own island! Must we face more empty houses because of the wealth of others? Must we lose more of our children to the mainland?"

Extract from letter written in reply:

YOUR REPLIES

Who does Burrowes think he is? Has he forgotten that he wasn't born on 'our' island? He came here twenty years ago on holiday and then bought a home! Doesn't he realise that the development of tourism is Goodbury's only hope for the future? Doesn't he realise that the tourists bring money onto the island? Over a hundred jobs are in tourism. How many of Port Goodbury's shops would survive without the tourists? Would the ferry survive without the tourists? This is the late 20th Century: what hope of new industry in Goodbury? None!"

A APPLICATION TO RE-OPEN GREY QUARRY

Grey Quarry was closed in 1982 with the loss of 66 jobs. Demand for granite has increased in recent years for use in flooring, patios etc. Local demand has also increased with the building developments proposed for Goodbury. An application has been made by a Cornish company to re-open the quarry.

Allowing this application to succeed will:
* Provide 44 temporary construction jobs (mostly to non-islanders).
* Provide an estimated 35 permanent quarry jobs (mostly to islanders).
* Assure the future of the port.

* Provide extra income for the island's shops and services.
* Provide extra money for the island through rate payments.
* Cause heavy lorries to use the island's roads.
* Cause dust pollution and noise of explosions.
* Increase the size of the unsightly quarry.

YOU MUST DECIDE whether to allow this application to proceed.

1 Describe in your own words the application, listing in two columns the advantages and disadvantages of the proposal.

2 If you do decide not to allow it to proceed, you must state your reasons for refusal clearly.

3 If you do allow the application to proceed, you must:
a) State clearly your reasons.
b) Enlarge the area of the quarry on the map by two squares.
c) Add two squares of housing to the built-up area of Port Goodbury.
d) Upgrade the road from the quarry to Port Goodbury.

B SERIOUS COASTAL EROSION AT PORT GOODBURY

Storm waves have concentrated their power on a point of weakness in the granite cliffs. A 2 metre section of the cliff top has fallen on to the beach, over a distance of about 20 m. This has covered a footpath and brought two cottages within a metre of the new cliff top.

1 What caused the cliff erosion at this point?

2 Mark the area on your map of Goodbury Island. It covers one square.

3 The council engineer presents you with two proposals:

PROPOSAL ONE Do nothing to prevent further cliff erosion. Pay compensation to the owners of the two cottages. Cost: £160 000.

PROPOSAL TWO Pour cement into the fault line, adding steel bracing. Build a small barrier wall at the base of the cliff. Cost: £110 000.

4 Consider the two proposals carefully. Make a list of the advantages and disadvantages of both proposals. Do not forget to consider the future as well as the present.

5 Decide which proposal to accept and justify your decision.

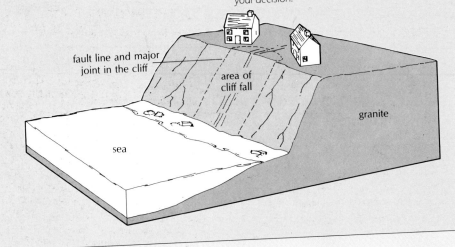

fault line and major joint in the cliff

area of cliff fall

granite

sea

C APPLICATION TO BUILD AN AIRSTRIP

An application has been received from the Victoria Hotel Company, owners of the island's largest hotel, to build an airstrip on Goodbury Island. Two alternative locations for the airstrip are proposed:

A Beside the coast road, 3 km NNW of Port Goodbury.
B 1 km south of St Bridget.

Average Weather Conditions

	SITE A	SITE B
Average windspeed (km/h)	34	19
Average annual rainfall (mm)	1350	890
Average days of fog a year	28	12
Average days of frost	75	88

Extract from letter printed in 'The Goodbury Globe', signed 'A Goodbury Resident':

Yet another daft proposal for our island. Building an airport so close to Port Goodbury will cause tremendous noise problems for the inhabitants. Add to that the traffic congestion and the danger – an airport is not needed here. Only the rich would use it anyway.

1 Mark the two alternative locations on your map.

2 List the advantages and disadvantages which an airstrip would bring to the island.

3 Draw up a table listing the advantages and disadvantages of both sites.

4 Decide whether the application should proceed and, if so, at which site. Give reasons for your decision.

5 If you decide to build the airstrip, add it to your map plus any other developments which you think would be necessary for the successful operation of the airstrip.

D APPLICATION TO BUILD A CONTAINER TERMINAL AT PORT GOODBURY

An application has been received from Land/Sea Containers plc of London to build a deep-water container terminal on the north shore of Goodbury Bay, immediately north of Port Goodbury. The increasing size of container vessels and the delays involved in shipping containers up the English Channel have encouraged Land/Sea Containers to propose the terminal at Port Goodbury to act as a transit point, or entrepôt. Large container vessels would berth at Port Goodbury and their cargo would be redistributed on to smaller vessels for onward transit to many smaller British and continental sea and river ports. A new breakwater would be built across Goodbury Bay and a broad deep-water jetty built out into the bay. A deep-water channel would have to be dredged into the harbour. There would be a large container storage area on the jetty. About 20 permanent jobs would be created.

1 Draw the proposed container terminal, breakwater and jetty on your map in pencil.

2 List the advantages and disadvantages of the proposal (think of the jobs created, both in construction and in the operation of the terminal, the extra income for the island, the visual impact and so on).

3 Decide whether the application should be allowed to proceed. Give the reasons for your decision.

4 If you have allowed the proposal to proceed, draw over the pencilled features on your map in ink.

E LANDSLIP AT ST BRIDGET

Four houses have collapsed following a landslip in the village of St Bridget. The landslip occurred west of the village, about a kilometre inland from the coast. The slopes above St Bridget at this point consist of clays and shales. The landslip followed a week of unusually heavy rain. The occupants of the houses had several minutes warning as the land began to slip slowly downhill. The only casualty was a Mr Ford who was slightly injured when his house collapsed while he was removing furniture. Insurance companies had refused to insure the houses because the area had been subject to subsidence in the past. The slope appears stable again now, but a dozen more houses could be threatened by further movements.

1 Mark the area of the landslip on your map. It covers two squares.

2 Study the diagrams below and say how the landslide occurred.

3 The council engineer has presented two proposals:

ONE Do nothing. Offer the threatened houseowners compensation. Cost: £600 000.

TWO Install a system of drains into the hillside to lead water away from the clay and prevent waterlogging. Build steel retaining walls into the slope to reduce movement. Cost: £400 000.

4 Consider the advantages and disadvantages of each proposal.

5 Decide what to do and justify your decision.

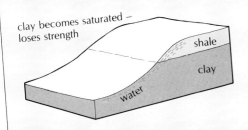

clay becomes saturated – loses strength

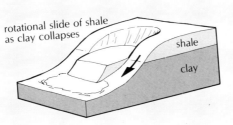

rotational slide of shale as clay collapses

G APPLICATION TO BUILD A HOLIDAY VILLAGE AT ST BRIDGET

An application has been received from Happy Days plc of Birmingham to build a holiday village at St Bridget. The site chosen is immediately north of the village, beside Bridget Bay. The village will consist of 50 holiday chalets, a caravan site for 30 permanent caravans, a bath and shower block, an indoor swimming pool, a small leisure centre and a supermarket. The village will be open from April to October each year. Local people will be able to use the swimming pool, leisure centre and supermarket during that period. This will provide useful services for the villagers. The holiday village will provide about 20 jobs during the season. Unemployment in St Bridget is the highest in the island.

1 Mark the area of the proposal on your map in pencil. It will cover six squares.

2 Make a list of the advantages and disadvantages of the proposal. What further developments would be needed once the village has been built? Think of electricity, water, sewerage and so on.

3 Decide whether the application should proceed. Justify your decision.

4 If you decide to allow the application to proceed, mark the holiday village on your map in ink.

H SERIOUS FLOODING OF THE RIVER MAWFORD AFFECTS PORT GOODBURY

The River Mawford flows through Port Goodbury to the sea. Following a month of very heavy rainfall, the river burst its banks and flooded two streets in the north of the town. Over 100 people were evacuated from their homes. Hydrographs of the river are available for study. These show changes in the river's response to heavy rainfall over the years. Some people blame the more efficient storm drains installed in Port Goodbury two years ago. Others blame the closure of Grey Quarry which used to extract water from the river.

1 Mark on your map the area of flooding. It covers four squares.

2 Make a copy of the hydrographs of the River Mawford. What do the hydrographs reveal about the river? What could be the cause be?

3 What steps can you take to prevent the flooding happening again? (Think of ways of increasing the river's velocity so that it can handle more water without overflowing.)

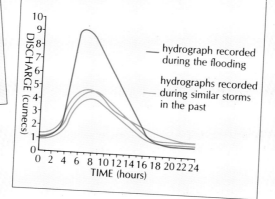

hydrograph recorded during the flooding

hydrographs recorded during similar storms in the past

F APPLICATION TO BUILD TEN RETIREMENT HOMES

An application has been received from local builder Patrick Tregorran to build ten bungalows for retired people immediately south of Port Goodbury, on land which has been considered a recreation ground for local children. Tregorran purchased the land last year. His wife is the Mayor of Port Goodbury. Tregorran has called on the council to provide a proper recreation ground for the town and has offered to contribute to the cost of developing it.

1 Mark the area of the proposal on your map in pencil. It will cover two squares.

2 Make a list of the advantages and disadvantages of the proposal. What further developments will be needed after the bungalows have been built?

3 Decide whether the application should proceed or not. Justify your decision.

4 If you decide to allow the application to proceed, mark the new estate on to your map in ink.

I APPLICATION TO BUILD A CRUDE OIL TERMINAL AT PORT GOODBURY

An application has been received from Celtic Petroleum of Cork, Irish Republic, to build a small terminal for crude oil at Port Goodbury. Exploration for oil in the Celtic Sea, between Goodbury Island and the Irish Republic, is proceeding and there are hopes of discovering oil in quantities sufficient to extract. At first, the terminal would handle imported crude oil from the Middle East, Africa and Venezuela. A new breakwater would be built across Goodbury Bay and a deep-water jetty constructed. Ten large oil storage tanks would be required. Efforts would be made to make the tanks blend in with the landscape of Port Goodbury. Large oil tankers would berth at Port Goodbury and smaller tankers would ship the crude oil on to refineries in Ireland, Britain and Europe. The terminal could be built on either the north or south side of Goodbury Bay. The terminal will provide eight permanent jobs.

1 Mark on your map the area of the terminal in pencil. It will cover two squares plus the jetty and breakwater.

2 Make a list of the advantages and disadvantages of the application.

3 Decide whether the application should proceed. Justify your decision.

4 If you decide to allow the application to proceed, mark the developments on your map in ink.

Poole

Bournemouth

Poole Harbour

Arne Peninsula

Sandbanks

South Haven Point

Studland Heath

Studland Bay

Swanage

Tilly Whim Caves

The picture opposite shows a stretch of the Dorset coast and how it is used by people. It is only 20 km between Bournemouth and Swanage, yet the coastline here is under intense pressure from many different land uses.

Tourism

The beaches of the area are among the best on the south coast, especially the broad, sandy beaches of Studland Bay. Bournemouth has grown from an empty heath in 1801 into one of Britain's largest seaside resorts. The Bournemouth section of the coast is now almost entirely built upon. Promenades, roads, cliff lifts, hotels, cafes, houses and beach huts cover the shore. Two pleasure piers extend Bournemouth's attractions out into the sea.

A million tourists visit Bournemouth each year. This section of the coastline is dominated by human use. The groynes on the beach, however, and the occasional cliff fall, reveal that nature has only been subdued, not beaten.

Bournemouth is a town which grew up because of tourism. The other major resort along this stretch of coastline is Swanage. Tourism is only a recent addition to Swanage; the town was once a fishing port and limestone quarrying centre. The old harbour, which used to export stone, is now full of pleasure craft. Power boats, yachts and wind surfers compete for space along this section of coast.

Urban Development

Bournemouth has grown so rapidly that it has swamped the older towns of Poole and Christchurch to form an urban area of over 300 000 people. Lack of planning control has allowed the attractive coastline to be built over. By the 1930s, when planning restrictions came into force, it was too late to conserve the natural coastline between Bournemouth and Sandbanks. Pressures were increasing for the development of the coast from South Haven Point to Swanage; but this stretch of coast has been largely preserved thanks to the efforts of local government and landowners, including the National Trust. Its future was assured in the 1970s, when it was designated as part of Britain's Heritage Coast.

Sewage Disposal

Sewage and industrial effluent are piped into the sea along this coast. Sometimes sewage is carried a few kilometres out by barge and dumped.

Shipping

Poole has been a small seaport for centuries. In recent years its importance has increased. Growing trade with Europe has led to the introduction of cargo ferry (roll on/roll off) services to Cherbourg. Land has been reclaimed from Poole Harbour to extend the docks.

Industry

The main industrial centre is Poole. Industries have developed around the port, including a power station whose chimneys dominate the skyline for many kilometres around. The industries use sea-water for cooling and some dispose of their effluent into the sea.

Mining

South of Swanage are the Tilly Whim Caves – the remains of limestone quarries which closed a century ago. More recently this coast has come under pressure from oil companies drilling for crude oil. The Wytch Farm Oilfield on the southern shores of Poole Harbour is Britain's largest onshore oilfield. There are six oil wells. Drilling has also taken place offshore.

Conservation

Many animals and plants live along this section of coast. Some are rare and protected, such as the Dartford warbler and the smooth snake. There is a large bird sanctuary on the Arne Peninsula. Studland Heath is one of the largest surviving areas of Dorset heathland.

1 *Name three attractions for tourists along this stretch of the Dorset coast.*

2 *Give three features which might discourage tourism.*

3 *Think of five other uses of the coast not described on these pages.*

4 *Design a brochure advertising holidays in Swanage. Remember to promote the area's attractions.*

5 *How do the various land uses along this section of coast compete and conflict?*

6 *An oil company has asked for planning permission to drill beneath the Arne Peninsula in Poole Harbour.*

  a) Form a group of four people who are among those attending a public enquiry on the oil company's drilling plans.

  b) Choose one of the following roles:
    ◦ A representative of the oil company.

    ◦ A representative of the Royal Society for the Protection of Birds.

    ◦ A member of Dorset County Council's Planning Authority.

    ◦ A member of the government's Department of Energy.

  c) Each group member should decide upon the views which she or he will adopt on the issue. You should prepare a detailed written description of your views.

  d) The group should then hold a discussion presenting each case in turn. Start with the oil company representative. Each member's case should be discussed.

  e) The member of the Department of Energy should then take on the extra role of chairperson and decide whether to allow the drilling to proceed or not. She or he must justify the decision to the other members.

1 Antarctica: a vast ice desert

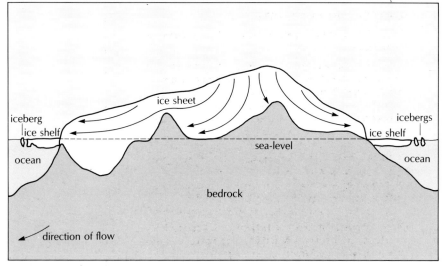

2 A cross-section through Antarctica (not shown to scale)

Visual 1 shows the bleak landscape of Antarctica, planet Earth's least hospitable place. This vast ice desert suffers from extreme cold and strong winds throughout much of the year. Winter temperatures regularly fall to −50 °C. It is a continent of ice, in places 4000 m thick. Ice covers one-tenth of the Earth's land area and 90% of that ice is in Antarctica.

The ice covering the Antarctic forms a great ice sheet. A cross-section through the ice sheet (Visual 2) reveals a dome of ice, with steep slopes at its margins and more gentle slopes towards the centre. The land is almost completely covered by ice. Only the highest mountains penetrate above the surface of the ice sheet. These mountains are called nunataks.

Ice is moving slowly outwards from the centre of the ice sheet. At its fastest the ice moves by a few hundred metres each year. The edge of the ice sheet is marked by an ice cliff, often over 30 m high. Blocks of ice break off the ice cliff to form icebergs. This process is called calving.

The Antarctic, a continent larger than Europe, is inhabited by a few hundred scientists. These come from 13 nations and they have established permanent bases in the Antarctic. An Antarctic Treaty came into operation in 1961. The treaty said that the whole continent should be used for scientific co-operation only for the next 30 years. Seven countries, including Britain, had claimed parts of the Antarctic as their territory. They agreed to suspend their claims while the treaty remained in force. No military activity or commercial developments were allowed. However, the treaty can be renegotiated in 1991. After that the scientists may be joined by miners, fishermen and soldiers. The Antarctic may have much to offer people. There are hopes of discovering and mining minerals. Tiny shrimps called krill inhabit the Antarctic waters by the billion. Some say that they could be the richest source of protein on Earth. Japan and Russia already catch the krill and many other nations may follow them.

At the North Pole the Arctic Ocean is ice-covered, but there is much more ice in the ice sheet which covers much of Greenland. The Greenland ice sheet is 3000 m thick at its maximum. It contains 8% of the world's ice. Smaller areas of ice called ice caps are found in Iceland (Vatnajökull) and Norway (Jostadalsbreen). These ice caps are between 500 and 750 m thick.

The Ice Age

At present there are two ice sheets in the world. In the past there were two others, one in North America and one in Europe. At that time almost a third of the Earth's land area was covered by ice. Recent research suggests that the Ice Age began between 2.5 and 3 million years ago and that there have been over 20 advances and retreats of the ice sheets. Visual 3 shows the area covered by the maximum extent of the ice sheets and Visual 4 shows a more detailed map of the Ice Age in Britain.

The last glaciers melted in Britain about 10 000 years ago. The Ice Age has not ended, however, since ice exists on the Earth today (for much of the Earth's history there have been no ice sheets at all). During the Ice Age, there have been periods called interglacials. The ice retreats and it becomes warmer during an interglacial. It is probable that we are currently in an interglacial period. In previous interglacials the temperature was higher than it is now and there was less ice around. It is known that the temperature of western Europe reached a maximum (called the climatic optimum) about 7000 years ago and has decreased since then. The fall in temperature may soon be enough to cause another glacial advance. It is thought, for example, that the current Norwegian ice cap is not a remnant of the Scandinavian ice sheet of earlier times. It could be a more recent development, following the fall in temperature since the climatic optimum.

The Earth is still a planet gripped by the Ice Age and one day the ice sheets may return to Britain.

1 *Write a sentence to describe each of these features:*

   a) ice sheet   b) ice cap   c) nunatak.

2 *Imagine that you are flying over the Antarctic on a clear day. Using the text and Visuals 1 and 2 write an account of what you might see. Use your atlas to help you.*

3 *a) How long ago did the Ice Age begin?*

   b) How many times during the Ice Age have the ice sheets advanced and retreated?

4 *What causes the ice sheets to advance and retreat?*

   a) Working with your neighbour, take each of the possible causes listed in the box. For each one discuss exactly why it might cause ice sheets to grow.

   b) Which possible cause or causes do you think is most likely? What are your reasons?

5 *It is possible that in the future part or all of the Antarctic ice sheet could melt. What effects might this have on:*
   a) Antarctica itself   b) the world as a whole?

6 *We are probably living in an interglacial period. The ice sheets are likely to return to parts of Britain and Europe. Working with your neighbour, say how you think a return of the ice sheets could affect people's lives.*

7 *Scientists think that ice sheets have advanced and retreated many times. What sort of evidence do you think they might use to prove this?*

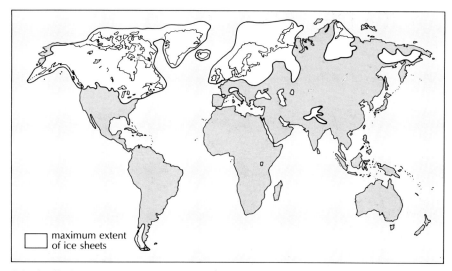

3 Ice Age Earth

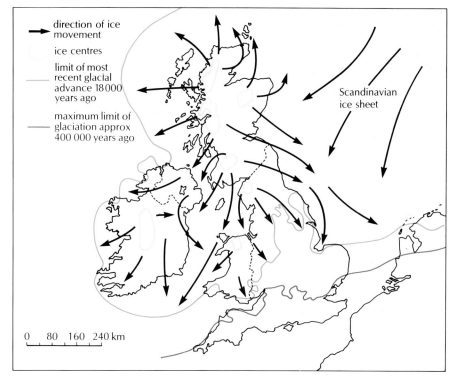

4 The Ice Age in Britain

WHAT CAUSES AN ICE AGE?

This is still a controversial question but the following factors may be important:

° Changes in the circulation of the atmosphere and the oceans. Winds and ocean currents help to circulate heat from the Equator towards the poles. It is thought that massive Earth movements, such as when mountains are formed, could change the heat circulation. This could reduce temperatures and increase snowfall in the polar regions.

° The Earth sometimes receives less heat from the sun due to:
  * a decrease in the sun's energy output caused by sun spots
  * an increase in cloud cover
  * an increase in atmospheric dust caused by volcanic eruptions
  * a change in the angle of tilt of the Earth's N–S axis
  * a change in the Earth's orbit, taking it further from the sun.

Once an ice sheet has developed it becomes self-supporting. Ice absorbs solar heat only slowly and so a large mass of ice tends to cool its surroundings and keep on freezing.

BEFORE GLACIATION

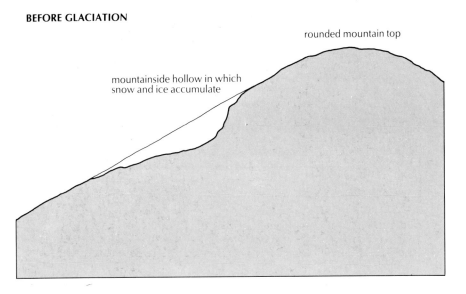

DURING GLACIATION

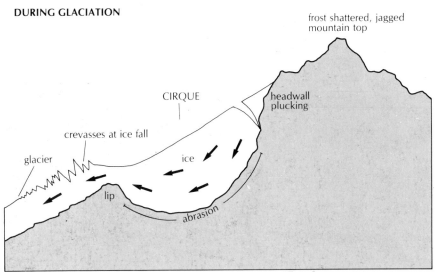

AFTER GLACIATION

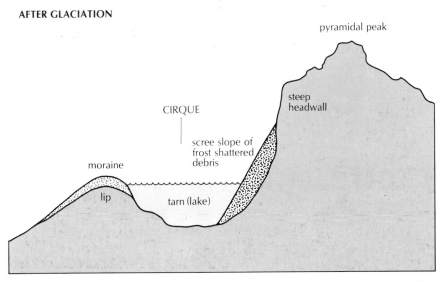

1 The formation of a cirque

As a climber ascends a mountain, she notices the air getting colder. If the mountain is high enough, the climber will pass the tree line. Above this no trees will grow. Higher still, the climber will reach the snow line. Above the snow line, snow and ice can be found all year round. The height of the snow line varies with the latitude of the mountain. In equatorial regions only the highest mountains rise above the snow line, which is about 6000 m above sea-level. In the Alps of southern Europe, the snow line is much lower, at about 3000 m. In southern Norway the snow line is at about 1000 m. It has been estimated that the snow line in Scotland would be at about 1500 m, if any mountains reached that height.

As the layers of snow build up, year by year, the lower layers are compressed. Air is forced out of the snow and it slowly turns to ice. As the ice grows it may begin to slide down the mountain under the pull of gravity. The ice has become a glacier. Most glaciers begin in mountainside hollows called cirques (Visual 1). Cirques begin as much smaller hollows which fill with snow. *Freeze/thaw* action increases the size of the hollow and, over many years, compression turns the snow into ice. A small hollow such as this is called a nivation hollow. As the ice in the hollow increases in depth it begins to slip, gouging out the hollow and creating a cirque.

Visual 3 shows the Rhône Glacier in Switzerland. The glacier flows from its source in the cirque (A), via the ice fall (B), to the valley below. The glacier flows down the valley until it reaches lower levels where the ice melts. The end of the glacier (C) is called the snout.

The Glacier System

Visual 5 shows the glacier system. The inputs to the glacier are snow and ice, which build up in the zone of accumulation. The output of the glacier is water (melted snow and ice). The melting of a glacier is called ablation. Accumulation is greatest in the winter and ablation is greatest in the summer. If there is more accumulation than ablation, the snout of the glacier will advance, and vice versa. The Rhône Glacier (Visual 3) has clearly retreated since it occupied more of the valley in the past.

FEATURES OF A GLACIER

Crevasses

Friction between the ice and the rock over which it moves makes the ice split and crevasses form. Crevasses may be several metres wide and up to 30 m deep. They can be lethal traps for people walking across a glacier, when covered by newly fallen snow.

Moraines

As a glacier moves across the landscape it collects rock fragments. The scattered debris of these rock fragments is called moraine. Some of the fragments fall on to the glacier from rocky slopes above. Some of them are torn away from the valley floor and sides by the ice freezing on to the rock. Such rock has to have been weakened before, perhaps by pressure or by freeze/thaw action. Moraine is transported by the glacier in a number of ways (Visual 2):

- Lateral moraine is carried along the edges of the glacier.
- Englacial moraine is carried within the ice . It may have fallen down crevasses, been washed down by streams flowing across the ice, or have melted its way down into the glacier.
- Ground moraine is moved along the bottom of the glacier.
- Medial moraine is formed where two glaciers join and their lateral moraines combine.

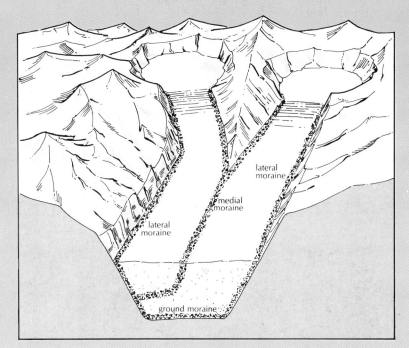

2 Cross-section through a glacier showing moraines

1 a) *Draw a simple cross-section of a 3500 m mountain in the Alps. Using dotted lines, add the tree line and snow line in the correct places.*

 b) *In your own words, say what the tree line and snow line are and why they vary from place to place.*

2 a) *How does snow turn into ice?*

 b) *What causes ice to slide downhill?*

 c) *Where do most glaciers begin?*

3 a) *What is the landform A on Visual 3?*

 b) *In your own words, with the aid of a diagram, say how it was formed.*

4 *Study Visual 4 and answer the following questions:*

 a) *What are accumulation and ablation?*

 b) *When is accumulation highest?*

 c) *When is ablation highest?*

5 a) *What evidence is there from Visual 3 to show that the Rhône Glacier has retreated?*

 b) *What might have caused the glacier to retreat?*

6 *How might glaciers such as the Rhône Glacier be useful to people?*

3 The Rhône Glacier

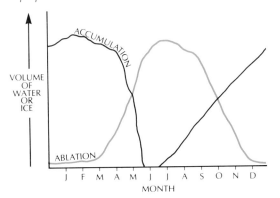

4 Accumulation and ablation over a year

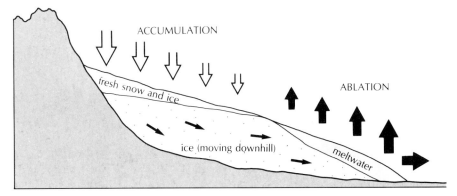

5 The glacier system

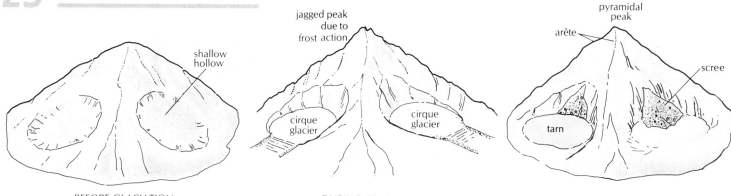

BEFORE GLACIATION   DURING GLACIATION   AFTER GLACIATION

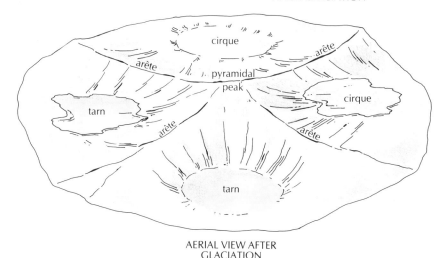

AERIAL VIEW AFTER
GLACIATION

1 The formation of arêtes and pyramidal peaks

Armed with fragments of rock called moraine, the glacial ice acts like a giant sheet of sandpaper, scratching and polishing the rock over which it passes. This process is called abrasion. Scratches called striations and smoothly polished surfaces called glacial pavements can be seen in many Lake District valleys today. Another common feature is the roche moutonée, formed where a more resistant outcrop of rock has been abraded by the ice.

FEATURES OF GLACIAL EROSION

Cirque

The eastern side of Helvellyn was the source area for a half-dozen glaciers whose cirques, including Red Tarn and Nethermost Cove, can be clearly seen today. Nethermost Cove forms an amphitheatre over 300 m deep. It has a narrow outlet to the east, through which the glacier flowed down a steep ice fall to Grisedale. After the Ice Age, lakes called tarns formed in many such cirques. Red Tarn is one such lake.

Arête

A cirque grows by erosion of the base and sides. Where two cirques have formed beside each other, there may be only a very narrow ridge of land separating them. Such a ridge is called an arête (Visual 1) and Striding Edge is an excellent example.

Pyramidal Peak

Where several cirques have eroded into a mountain from all sides they may form a pyramidal peak or horn (Visual 1). At Helvellyn there are no cirques on the western side of the mountain, so it is not a pyramidal peak. Perhaps the best example of a pyramidal peak is the Matterhorn in the Swiss Alps.

Glacial Trough

If there is enough ice behind it, a glacier may move downhill. It may flow over the lip of the cirque and follow the line of a river valley down the mountainside. The glacier whose source was Nethermost Cove flowed northeastwards along Grisedale and joined the large glacier in Patterdale. This small tributary glacier from Nethermost Cove had great erosive power. Grisedale was changed from a winding river valley into a straight, deep glacial valley (Visual 3). The interlocking spurs of the river valley were removed. The V-shaped cross-section of the river valley was replaced with an open U-shaped cross-section as the glacier eroded deeply into the mountainside. The valley sides of Grisedale rise sharply over 400 m above the valley floor. Some glacial troughs, such as the fjords of Norway, may be up to 3000 m deep. Glacial troughs are not smooth. There are deeper rock basins, rock barriers and rock steps. After the ice has retreated, the rock basins may be occupied by long, narrow lakes called ribbon lakes. An example is Lake Ullswater. Patterdale has been largely occupied by Ullswater, which is in places over 70 m deep.

1 If you were walking along a glacial valley, what evidence would you look for to show that the valley had been formed by moving ice?

2 Study Visual 2 which is of High Street in the Lake District. Like the Helvellyn area, it has been mainly shaped by ice.

   a) Name the landform running from A to B.

   b) Name the type of lake at C and D.

   c) Name the landforms at E and F.

   d) For all the landforms identified above, give one named example from the Helvellyn area.

3 Using the other Visuals to help you, draw your own diagrams to explain how the landforms E and F (on Visual 2) were formed by ice.

4 The landscape of the Lake District has been slowly changing since the ice melted. Look again at Visual 2. What do you think is happening at G?

5 In the Lake District the cirques face in different directions of the compass, as the table below shows. One way of plotting this is to use this polar graph:

2 High Street and Blea Water, Lake District

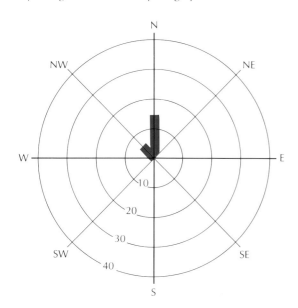

number of cirques

0   10   20   30   40

   a) Complete the polar graph.

   b) Describe the pattern that your graph shows.

   c) Suggest some reasons why there are more cirques facing in some directions than in others.

COMPASS DIRECTION	PERCENTAGE OF CIRQUES
N	16
NE	39
E	20
SE	15
S	3
SW	1
W	1
NW	5

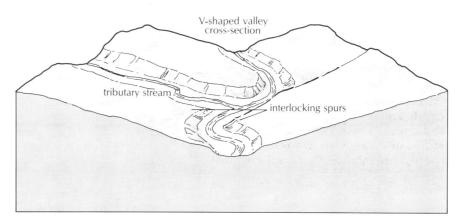

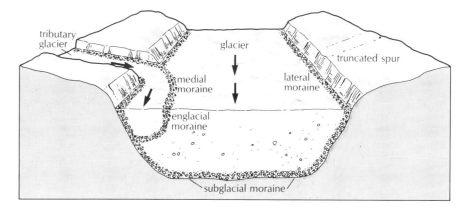

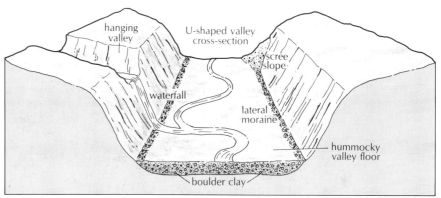

3 The formation of a U-shaped valley

ASSIGNMENT SEVEN

Glacial Scenery in the Lake District

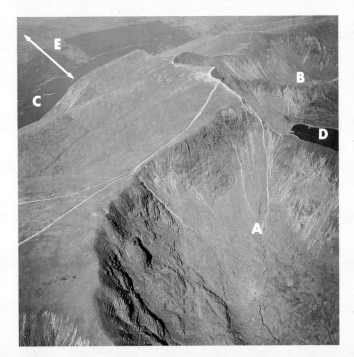

1 Helvellyn, Lake District

The walk from Glenridding, on the shores of Ullswater, to the summit of Helvellyn is one of the most spectacular which the Lake District can offer. Starting from a height of 200 m, the road soon becomes a track climbing the ridge above Grisedale. It is a steep and steady climb giving increasingly impressive views of Patterdale and Lake Ullswater. Ahead, the summit of Helvellyn is hidden by the lie of the land, until the track reaches about 600 m. Soon the track becomes a narrow path, as little as a metre wide in places, with steep slopes falling away over 300 m on either side. This narrow ridge is called Striding Edge. The wind always blows keenly across Striding Edge, threatening the walker with a swift descent to the waters of Red Tarn to the north or the rocky hollow of Nethermost Cove to the south. Once Striding Edge has been safely crossed it is a short climb to the summit of Helvellyn, at 950 m above sea-level. If you are lucky enough to climb on a clear day, the views from the summit are superb. It is possible to see almost the whole of the Lake District.

The spectacular scenery of the Helvellyn area is due to several factors. The whole Lake District area was pushed up by great earth movements many millions of years ago. Since then some rocks have been worn away; while others, being harder and stronger, have resisted erosion and weathering. However, the most important event in shaping this landscape was undoubtedly the Ice Age.

Your Assignment

In this assignment you are going to use the following skills:

○ Answering questions on a descriptive passage.
○ Interpreting an Ordnance Survey map.
○ Drawing a cross-section.
○ Interpreting an aerial photograph.

Resources

1 Visuals 1 and 2.
2 Extract from guide.

Work Programme A

Study the Ordnance Survey 1:50 000 map extract (Visual 2) and answer the following questions:

1 What do the symbols at the following grid references represent: i) 377169 ii) 366174   iii) 351147   iv) 386169?

2 Give the correct grid reference for the following: i) the summit of The Cape   ii) the mountain rescue post in Glenridding   iii) Grisedale Tarn iv) the two islands in Thirlmere.

3 Name the landforms shown at the following grid references, choosing from the list below: i) 348120 ii) 370150   iii) 360179   iv) 310170 v) 343160.

cirque	tarn
U-shaped valley	ribbon lake
arête	hanging valley.

Work Programme B

1 Follow, on the map extract, the route described in the text. Still following the route, calculate the distance (to the nearest kilometre) from Glenridding (grid reference 387174) to the summit of Helvellyn (342152).

2 Draw a cross-section from 347160 to 347140. Present the section on graph paper, using a vertical scale of 1 mm = 10 m.
  Write the following labels in the correct places on your cross-section:

Red Tarn	arête
Striding Edge	cirque.
Nethermost Cove	

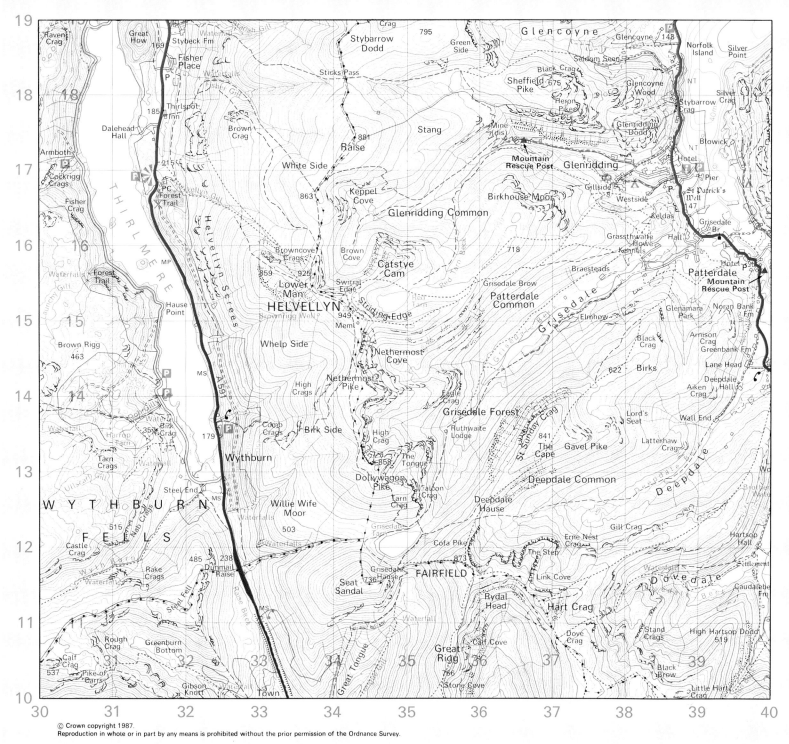

2 Extract from the Ordnance Survey map of the Helvellyn area (scale 1:50 000)

Work Programme C

Using the aerial photograph (Visual 1):

1 Name the landforms (not the places) labelled A to E.

2 Draw or trace a labelled sketch of the view shown in the photograph, using the real place names.

3 Describe in your own words the glacial landform at D. How has it been formed?

Work Programme D

1 What evidence is there, from the map and the photograph, that Helvellyn is an area heavily used by tourists?

2 Footpath erosion is a considerable problem in the area. What could be done to reduce this?

LANDFORMS OF GLACIAL DEPOSITION

Terminal Moraine

At the snout of the glacier (or ice sheet), moraine falls from the melting ice to form a ridge – called a terminal or end moraine. Many glaciated valleys have terminal moraines stretching across them, often now reduced to a line of hummocks dissected by streams. The terminal moraines of ice sheets are much larger landforms. The Cromer Ridge in Norfolk marks the limit of an ice sheet moving southwards across the North Sea. In places over 100 m high, the Cromer Ridge includes boulders and stones from the nearby chalklands, as might be expected. More surprising are the rocks from the north of England, Scotland and even Norway which can be found within the Cromer Ridge. Such rocks have been carried by ice to an area far from their point of origin and are called erratics.

Recessional Moraine

The retreat of a glacier or ice sheet was rarely a smooth or rapid event. Usually the ice retreated in stages, sometimes with small advances as well. If the ice halted for long enough during its retreat, another terminal moraine might be formed. Such a moraine is called a recessional moraine; there may be several marking points along its line of retreat where the ice halted.

Lateral Moraine

In some glaciated valleys a terrace of moraine can be seen running along the valley side. This is the lateral moraine, formed at the sides of the glacier by rocks falling on to the ice from the slopes above. As the ice melted, the moraine subsided to its present position.

Drumlin

In the Eden Valley, east of the Lake District, are many low, rounded hillocks called drumlins. A drumlin lies parallel to the direction of ice flow with its steeper slope facing up-glacier. The drumlins in the Eden Valley are 10–50 m in height and 50–500 m in length. A group of drumlins is called a swarm and the resulting hummocky landscape is sometimes called 'basket of eggs' topography. Most drumlins consist only of boulder clay. Nobody is sure how drumlins are formed. It is thought that ground moraine has been shaped into drumlins by ice flowing over it. The streamlined shape of the drumlins reflects the wave-like movement of the ice.

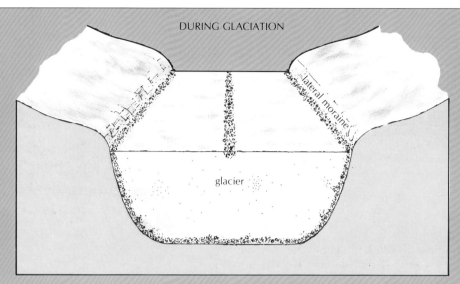

DURING GLACIATION

lateral moraine

glacier

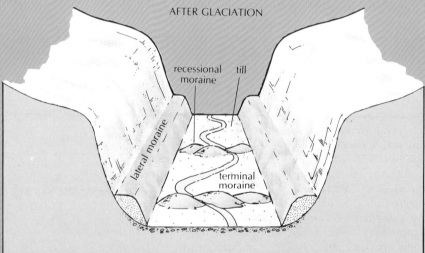

AFTER GLACIATION

recessional moraine

till

lateral moraine

terminal moraine

ice

DRUMLIN

boulder clay

Crag and Tail

Some drumlins have cores of solid rock. Their formation may be similar to the crag and tail found in Edinburgh. Castle Rock is a crag of very resistant basalt rock which withstood the passage of a glacier. In the lee of the crag a tail of weaker sedimentary rock has survived, protected from erosion by the ice. The Royal Mile runs along the gently sloping tail, leading up to the crag on which is perched Edinburgh Castle.

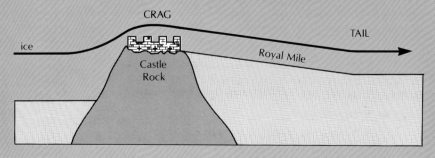

CRAG

TAIL

ice

Royal Mile

Castle Rock

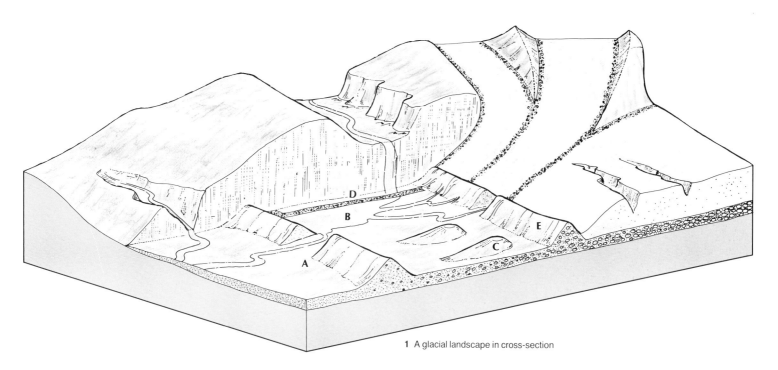

1 A glacial landscape in cross-section

The highlands of Britain, such as the Lake District, bear the scars of glacial erosion. They also show the process of glacial deposition. The load of a glacier will be dropped where the ice melts. This is mainly at the snout of the glacier, but it can also occur underneath or at the sides of the glacier. Glacial drift is the general term given to these glacial deposits. Some of the main depositional landforms are outlined in the visuals on these pages.

Glacial drift is of two types, depending on whether it has been deposited by ice or water. Ground moraine (also known as till or boulder clay) is the most common type of drift, covering large areas of central and northern Britain. Ground moraine has been deposited by ice. It is an unsorted jumble of rock fragments which are jagged and angular. These are very different from river deposits. It is usually easy to tell whether particles have been deposited by ice or water because river deposits at any one place tend to be of roughly the same size. Also, the rocks deposited by rivers are rounded and smoothed by the water. River deposits are found in layers (or strata), each marking a particular period of deposition.

1 Read through the information on these pages. Then, using Visual 1:

   a) Identify landforms A to E.

   b) Explain the difference between a terminal moraine and a recessional moraine.

2 Study the sections through two deposits (Visual 2).

   a) Which do you think has been deposited by ice and which by water?

   b) Give three reasons to explain your choice.

3 a) In your own words say what a drumlin is.

   b) How does a drumlin differ from a crag and tail? Illustrate your answer with two labelled diagrams.

4 a) What is an erratic rock?

   b) How do you think the study of erratics would help in understanding the direction and speed of movement of ice sheets?

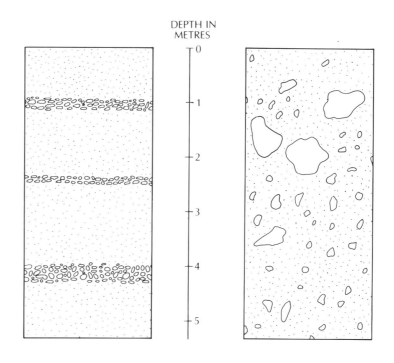

2 Two deposits seen in vertical section

MELTWATER LANDFORMS (FLUVIO-GLACIAL)

Outwash Plain
Outwash plains may stretch for hundreds of km from the ice front. They consist of sands and gravels carried by meltwater streams from glacial moraine. The surface of the plain is often hummocky and cut by several wide, braided, meltwater channels. Sometimes there may be small ponds called kettle holes. These have formed where blocks of dead ice slowly melted, leaving depressions in the outwash. The outwash plain is sorted because the larger rocks are deposited first and the finer material is carried much further. The outwash will also be in layers (stratified), with each layer representing the material deposited during one season's ice melt.

Esker
An esker is a long, narrow, winding ridge of sand and gravel. It may meander for several km across a glaciated area and may be up to 15 m high. It marks the course of a subglacial stream channel and represents the deposition of sediment on the channel floor.

Kame
A kame is a small mound of sand and gravel. It may be formed by material deposited in crevasses by meltwater streams flowing across the surface of the ice. As the ice melts, the material subsides to the ground.

Kame Terrace
A kame terrace is formed by the build up of sediment in meltwater lakes at the glacier's edge. After glaciation, the kame terrace appears as a ridge running along the valley side. It may be confused with a lateral moraine, but analysis of the material should easily reveal its true identity.

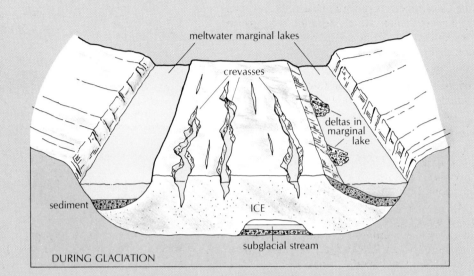

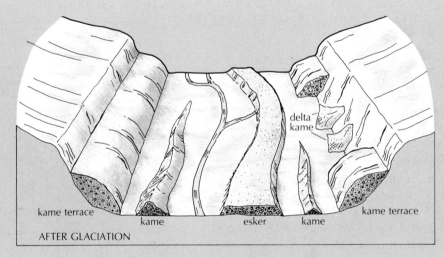

On a fine summer's day, walking and climbing in the mountains can be a warm business. Places which would be very cold in winter can have high temperatures during the day in summer. This seasonal difference in temperature affects mountain glaciers.

Ice can melt anywhere along the glacier, although the rate of melting (or ablation) is greatest towards the snout. Rates of ablation vary throughout the year, reaching a maximum on summer afternoons.

Melting glaciers release large amounts of meltwater. This may form streams flowing on top or along the side of the ice. Meltwater can disappear down crevasses and then flow in tunnels inside or below the glacier. These streams often flow under a great pressure, and at a high speed. This means that they can carry a large load of rock particles. When the meltwater reaches the glacier snout, it usually slows down and drops much of its load, thus changing the landscape by deposition.

Meltwater Landforms
The melting and formation of ice are not merely seasonal. They happen on a much larger scale, as the climate becomes warmer or colder. At the height of the Ice Age, ice (hundreds of metres thick) covered enormous areas. So much of the Earth's rain and snow water was locked up in the ice sheets that the sea-level fell by 50 m. That drop of 50 m was felt all over the world! It produced a vast amount of meltwater when the climate warmed up and the ice sheets began to melt. No wonder that meltwater has created some important landforms. Some of them are explained in the box above.

How Meltwater Affects River Systems

The melting of ice sheets can sometimes have a big influence on the course of rivers. Take Britain's longest river, the Severn, as an example. The Severn rises on the slopes of Plynlimon in central Wales, as Visual 1 shows. Follow the path taken by the river. It flows north east for over 40 km, heading for the Irish Sea. Then, unexpectedly, instead of flowing across the lowland to the north, the Severn turns sharply south towards the Shropshire Hills. It then cuts its way through a steep-sided gorge at Ironbridge and flows southwards for over 100 km to enter the sea through the Bristol Channel.

The strange course of the River Severn cannot be explained by present day conditions. Logically it should end up flowing into the Irish Sea after flowing northwards. Indeed, in the past this is just what it did. What happened?

About 16 000 years ago an ice sheet, moving in from the Irish Sea, blocked the Severn's exit to the sea. Water was trapped between the ice front and the high ground of the Shropshire Hills. A large lake was formed (called Lake Lapworth after the person who first identified it). Lake Lapworth filled up until the water began to overflow over the lowest point in the Shropshire Hills, at Ironbridge. Water flowing through this glacial overflow channel formed the deep gorge found there today. The River Severn still flows southwards through the gorge, even though its original course is available again.

1 The table on the right shows the discharge of one meltwater stream during a 24-hour period.

a) Draw a line graph to show how the discharge changes over the 24 hours. Put the hours along the bottom of your graph and the discharge figures up the side.

b) Describe the pattern that your graph shows.

c) Try to explain the pattern.

2 The table bottom right shows how the average discharge of the same meltwater stream changes from month to month over a year.

a) Draw a bar graph to show the monthly changes.

b) Describe the pattern shown by the graph and try to explain it.

3 Check with the information given here before you answer these questions:

a) You have found a ridge of sand and gravel deposits at the edge of a valley. Is this likely to be a kame terrace or an esker? Why?

b) What happens to the size of rock particles in an outwash plain as you move away from the ice front? Why does this happen?

c) You have found rounded rock particles close to the ice front. What has happened to these particles?

4 What happened to the River Severn is called glacial diversion of drainage. Explain how the Severn was diverted from its previous course by drawing a series of three simple sketch maps.

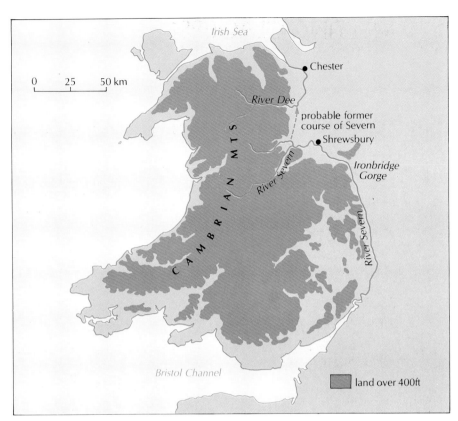

1 The diversion of the River Severn

DISCHARGE OF A MELTWATER STREAM DURING A 24-HOUR PERIOD

Time (hours)	Discharge (cubic metres per second)	Time (hours)	Discharge (cubic metres per second)
0100	0.4	1300	3.8
0200	0.4	1400	4.5
0300	0.4	1500	4.7
0400	0.3	1600	4.4
0500	0.3	1700	3.7
0600	0.4	1800	2.8
0700	0.5	1900	1.9
0800	0.7	2000	1.4
0900	1.0	2100	0.9
1000	1.4	2200	0.6
1100	1.9	2300	0.5
1200	2.9	2400	0.4

ANNUAL DISCHARGE OF A MELTWATER STREAM

Month	Average discharge (cubic metres per second)	Month	Average discharge (cubic metres per second)
January	0.2	July	3.8
February	0.2	August	3.7
March	0.5	September	3.1
April	1.1	October	2.0
May	2.0	November	0.8
June	3.2	December	0.3

1 The 'English Prairies'

East Anglia is underlain mainly by chalk. Elsewhere in southern England the chalk forms downland, rising to 300 m, with steep scarp slopes and deep dry valleys. Yet East Anglia is a region of low-lying, gently undulating land which barely reaches 100 m in height. Why the difference? The answer lies in the effect of the Ice Age.

East Anglia was covered by an ice sheet at least four times during the Ice Age. The whole region is covered by glacial deposits.

A thick layer of ground moraine, over 140 m thick in places, lies over much of the area. This ground moraine is called chalky boulder clay. Over 300 square km of chalky boulder clay has been deposited as a result of the erosion of the chalk scarp. It is estimated that the scarp has been eroded by up to 14 km eastwards of its original position (before the Ice Age). A deep and fertile soil has formed on the chalky boulder clay. The heavier clay soils have dairy cattle pastures. The less heavy soils have arable crops. Recently, hedgerows have been uprooted to form large fields suitable for the intensive use of big combined harvesters and *vining machines*. There are now vast wheat and barley fields (the so-called 'English Prairies'), and fields of sugar beet, potatoes and rape.

One of the later ice sheets only reached northern Norfolk. The point where it stopped is marked by a large terminal moraine, the Cromer Ridge (Visuals 2 and 3). This extends for over 15 km from near Cromer to Holt. The ridge is over 100 m high in places, rising steeply from the coastal lowland, but dipping away more gently to the south. Bracken and heather cover the soil, which consists of sand and gravel.

Meltwater streams flowed southwards from the Cromer Ridge terminal moraine. They carried fine sand and silt, which they deposited over a wide area as outwash. The Goodsands area of north west Norfolk was once poor sheep pasture, but it has been improved by fertilizers and soil conditioners. Peas, carrots and cabbages are grown in addition to wheat and barley (Visual 4). The sands and gravels of the Breckland support heathland with coniferous plantations. Vegetables are grown on improved soils. The fertile loam soils of north east Norfolk have also formed from outwash deposits. Wheat and sugar beet were the most important crops here, until the increased demand for frozen foods led to a change to peas and beans. This shows that economic factors are now much more important to farmers than physical factors. Much of the finer sand and silt of the outwash deposits has been blown away by the wind and deposited elsewhere in southern East Anglia. Such wind-blown deposits are called loess or brick earth.

2 The steep slope of the Cromer Ridge behind Weybourne

3 The Cromer Ridge south of Sheringham

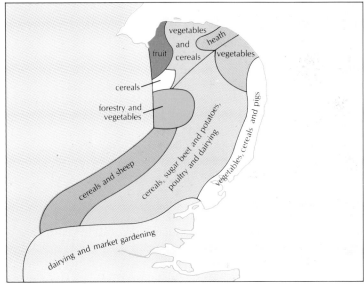

4 Farming regions in East Anglia

The cliffs of northern Norfolk are made up of glacial sands, clays and gravels. Large masses of chalk, some hundreds of metres long, can be seen in the cliffs. These were eroded from the chalk scarp and deposited by the ice sheet, several kilometres from their original place.

1 *Rocks from as far away as Norway have been found in the surface deposits of East Anglia. What are such rocks called and how have they got there?*

2 *Study Visual 5.*

   a) *Describe the line of the chalk scarp on the map. What does the dashed line represent?*

   b) *How has the line of the scarp been altered?*

3 a) *What is chalky boulder clay?*

   b) *Describe the area that the chalky boulder clay covers.*

   c) *How was the chalky boulder clay formed?*

   d) *How has chalky boulder clay influenced farming?*

4 a) *Describe the Cromer Ridge.*

   b) *How was the Cromer Ridge formed?*

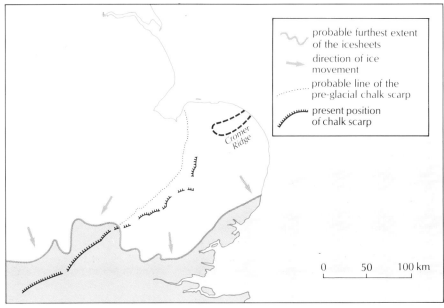

5 How the Ice Age affected East Anglia

High in the Swiss Alps the air is clear and cool. More importantly, for the Swiss tourist industry, the snow in the Alps is deep and extensive. Almost half the tourists visiting Switzerland go for winter holidays. The travel agents' shelves are packed with brochures offering winter sports at exciting-looking resorts. One of the most famous – and most expensive – is Zermatt (opposite). Zermatt was a small farming village before the growth of winter holidays changed its character forever. February and March are the busiest months, but throughout the year tourists are attracted by the spectacular mountain scenery. However, across the Swiss Alps as a whole, hotel beds are occupied for only 120 days a year. This under-use of the facilities loses money and means that many people working in tourism are unemployed for several months of the year. Chalets for rent and sale have been built around many resorts, but most of them are occupied for only a couple of months during the winter.

The Alpine environment is fragile. Some people say that the presence of millions of skiers is damaging it. Litter, noise and erosion are caused by the tourists. The ski lifts, ski tows and cable cars scar the mountain scenery. The hotels, chalets, restaurants, indoor swimming pools, shops and car parks bring concrete cities and urban life styles into this once remote and peaceful landscape. Even the cool and clear air now carries a threat to the Alps. One in five of the trees of the Alpine forests is dying, hit by the effects of acid rain. The trout have died in many of the smaller lakes, killed by the rising levels of acidity. Will the Alps survive the onslaught of modern society?

1 a) Describe the location of Zermatt in relation to the physical features of the area.

  b) What is the Matterhorn an example of?

2 Study the opposite page and answer the following:

  a) Which mountain dominates the village of Zermatt?

  b) Why is it safe to 'amble peacefully along the street' in Zermatt?

  c) What route would you take to ski into Italy? Which Italian village could you reach?

  d) List ten things that Zermatt offers tourists who do not ski.

3 Study the opposite page and answer the following:

  a) List five facilities of the Hotel Ambassador.

  b) How much would the following holidays in Zermatt cost you:

   i) 7 nights at the Hotel Ambassador from 28 January, travelling by car?

   ii) 14 nights at the Hotel Ambassador from 11 February, by air?

   iii) 7 nights at the Hotel Tschugge from 3 March, by air?

  c) Which Swiss airport do you fly to for Zermatt?

  d) How do you transfer from the airport to Zermatt, and how long does the transfer take?

  e) How much does it cost (in £ sterling) to hire skis and boots for six days? (The exchange rate is 3 Swiss Francs = 1 pound.)

  f) How much does the ski school cost for six days?

  g) How much is a lift pass for 13 days?

4 The table below shows the countries of origin of tourists visiting Zermatt:

COUNTRY OF ORIGIN	% OF TOTAL FOREIGN TOURISTS
West Germany	42
USA	11
Netherlands	9
UK	9
France	8
Belgium	5
Sweden	4
Spain	2
Others	11

  a) Using the map of Europe, find a way of showing where tourists visiting Switzerland come from.

  b) Why do you think that there are few tourists from Switzerland's neighbours, Austria and Italy?

5 The table below shows how people in the Swiss Alpine resort of Flumserburg are employed in tourism:

Hotels, entertainment	46%
Shops	12%
Ski school	8%
Lifts	9%
Public services	8%
Building	7%
Others	10%

  a) Draw a bar graph or a pie chart to show these figures.

  b) Which jobs will not be available throughout the year? How is this a problem?

6 a) What are the benefits of winter tourism in the Alps?

  b) How might the natural environment of the Alps be disturbed by such developments?

  c) Should the development of tourism in environments like the Alps be controlled? If so, how could it be done? Who would benefit? Who would suffer?

ZERMATT

Zermatt is one of the world's leading ski resorts and, in our opinion, the most picturesque village in the Alps, dominated by the majestic Matterhorn and surrounded by numerous mountain peaks and glaciers. The village is compact and no cars are allowed in, so skiers and non-skiers can amble peacefully along the street, only occasionally giving way to a horse-drawn sleigh or an electro-taxi.

SKIERS
Skiing possibilities are endless, particularly for intermediates and experts who can get the most advantage from the long and at times, challenging descents.

From the Stockhorn area, it is possible to get from one area to another without returning to the village and novices and experts alike can enjoy the gentle slopes of the Theodul glacier. From the Kleine Matterhorn, at 12,500 ft, you can ski over to the Plateau Rosa and on down the delightful Ventina run to Cervinia on the Italian side of the Matterhorn. Experienced skiers may well like to try helicopter skiing and sample the really deep off-piste snow on the Monte Rosa.

CHILDREN
Youngsters are well catered for in Zermatt: the Kinderheim Theresia will take infants from 3 months old to 8 years, there are qualified nursery nurses as well as ski instructors for the older children. Cost for 6 days is about 200 SF, to include lunch and a snack.

NON-SKIERS
Although Zermatt is essentially a skiers resort, it has plenty of attractions for non-skiing winter visitors. There is skating, curling, ice-hockey, tobogganing, beautiful walks, swimming and sauna baths, and everyone can go up the Gornergrat rack railway, or in one of the numerous cable cars to enjoy the sun and magnificent scenery. The mountains are dotted with restaurants, so there is no need to go hungry or thirsty.

APRÈS-SKI
Après-ski is plentiful with something for everyone. Elsie's Bar and The Brown Cow are popular meeting places and at the other end of the scale there is dancing to a group in the Zermatterhof Bar. The group in the Matterhorn Stube of the Hotel Mont Cervin are very popular, and the best discos are 'Le Village de la Poste' and the 'Pollux' which is chic and friendly and interchanges disco music with a live group.

YOUR HOTEL CHOICE IN ZERMATT
Hotel Ambassador
* Free Swimming Pool.

A luxury class hotel, barely 4 minutes from the Gornergrat station, with a large indoor swimming pool (free for guests), sauna, massage and a games room. The hotel is beautifully furnished, it has a comfortable lounge bar, two restaurants, and the cuisine is highly recommended. All bedrooms have bath, wc and mini-bar. New Year's Eve Gala dinner is included in our prices.

TÄSCH/ZERMATT

ALL PRICES PER PERSON IN £'s PS = Shower PB = Bath

Resort	TÄSCH						ZERMATT					
Hotel/Apartment	MONTE ROSA (SELF CATERING)						GORNERGRAT		TSCHUGGE		AMBASSADOR	
Holiday Code	6040		6041		6042		6172		6171		6173	
Prices include	Studio 2 pers. occ.		2 Rooms 4 pers. occ.		3 Rooms 6 pers. occ.		Bed & Breakfast Bath & WC.		Half Board PB. or PS. & WC.		Half Board Bath & WC.	
Travel	🚗 ⛷		🚗 ⛷		🚗 ⛷		🚗 ⛷		🚗 ⛷		🚗 ⛷	
Duration in nights	7	14	7	14	7	14	7	14	7	14	7	14
Dec 17	63	–	124	–	62	–	123	–	56	–	117	–	127	–	188	–	164	–	215	–	190	–	250	–
Dec 24	–	198	–	259	–	175	–	236	–	157	–	218	–	326	–	387	–	389	–	450	–	517	–	578
Jan 7.14.21	67	95	128	156	62	87	123	148	61	78	122	139	137	227	198	288	172	288	233	349	205	375	265	436
Jan 28	71	129	132	190	68	101	129	162	62	94	127	155	147	254	208	325	177	304	238	365	214	387	274	448
Feb 4	78	154	139	215	81	114	142	175	76	103	137	164	164	274	225	335	189	334	250	395	222	407	282	468
Feb 11	87	162	148	223	88	124	149	185	73	120	134	181	178	284	239	345	204	354	265	415	231	434	292	495
Feb 18.25	100	168	161	229	96	146	157	207	87	128	148	189	191	314	252	375	225	367	286	428	254	474	315	535
Mar 3	87	138	148	199	86	126	147	187	76	102	137	163	171	284	232	345	204	327	265	388	228	427	289	488
Mar 10	83	123	144	184	75	116	136	177	67	87	128	148	164	266	225	327	194	317	255	378	217	397	277	458
Mar 17	63	95	124	156	62	87	123	148	56	78	117	139	137	243	198	304	164	297	225	358	195	375	255	436
Mar 24.31	67	103	128	164	67	94	128	155	64	83	125	144	146	247	207	308	174	307	235	368	205	384	265	445
Apr 7	63	118	124	179	62	116	123	177	56	91	117	152	137	264	198	325	164	321	225	382	195	417	255	478
Apr 14	81	–	142	–	83	–	144	–	74	–	135	–	164	–	225	–	198	–	259	–	224	–	285	–
Additional options Price per person per week. Other durations pro rata.	Single occ. £4		3 pers. occ. £15 2 pers. occ. £27		5 pers. occ. £9		Single occ. £14 Half Board £49		Single occ. £14		Single occ. £35	

CAR SUPPLEMENTS PER PERSON: 4 in car £3. 3 in car £5. 2 in car £10. (Prices above apply to 5 or more in car)

TRAVEL INFORMATION
BY AIR:
Day flights to Geneva from Gatwick and Manchester. Onward transfers by coach to Täsch and then by mountain rail to Zermatt. For provincial airport supplement and full details see page 6.

BY CAR:
For full details see page 6.

SKI PACK
ZERMATT (also for Täsch guests)
Not pre-bookable

Ski Hire	6 days SF 69	13 days SF 112
Boot Hire	6 days SF 39	13 days SF 54
Ski School	(4 hours daily) 6 days SF 115	
Lift Pass	(whole area) 6 days SF 196 13 days SF 346	

For further details see page 65

1 Volcanic eruption: Mauna Loa, Hawaii

The Earth can kill. In Britain we are used to a stable land. We say that things are 'as safe as houses' or 'as old as the hills'. In some parts of the world, the houses are not safe, and the hills are not old. Earthquakes can smash your house and volcanic eruptions can bury it. In the past people spoke of the rage of the gods and the fires of hell to explain the frightening mysteries of earthquake and volcano. We know now that neither gods nor devils come into it; the real killer is the planet itself. Our understanding is improving all the time. As recently as the 1960s scientists studying the Earth were faced with many problems which they could not easily explain:

○ Volcanoes and earthquakes occur only in certain places on the Earth's surface. These areas tend to be in narrow belts or bands such as the 'ring of fire' surrounding the Pacific Ocean.

○ Great ranges of *fold mountains* occur in the same land areas as the volcanoes and earthquakes.

○ There is evidence of a former ice age 290 million years ago which covered much of Antarctica, South Africa, South America, India and Australia. The ice movements which have been reconstructed reveal no pattern, simply chaos.

○ The fossils of identical species of plants and animals have been discovered in widely separated continents. They include dinosaurs, which could not possibly have swum across the oceans separating the places where their fossils have been found.

○ The ancient fossils and rocks of Australia are very similar to those of Africa and India. During the last 150 million years, Australia has developed its own species and rocks.

○ Studies of the ocean bed reveal very deep, narrow trenches running along some of the major earthquake belts. Volcanic ridges are also found running along some of the major volcanic belts of the Earth.

What was the answer to these mysteries?

2 The Earth's crustal plates

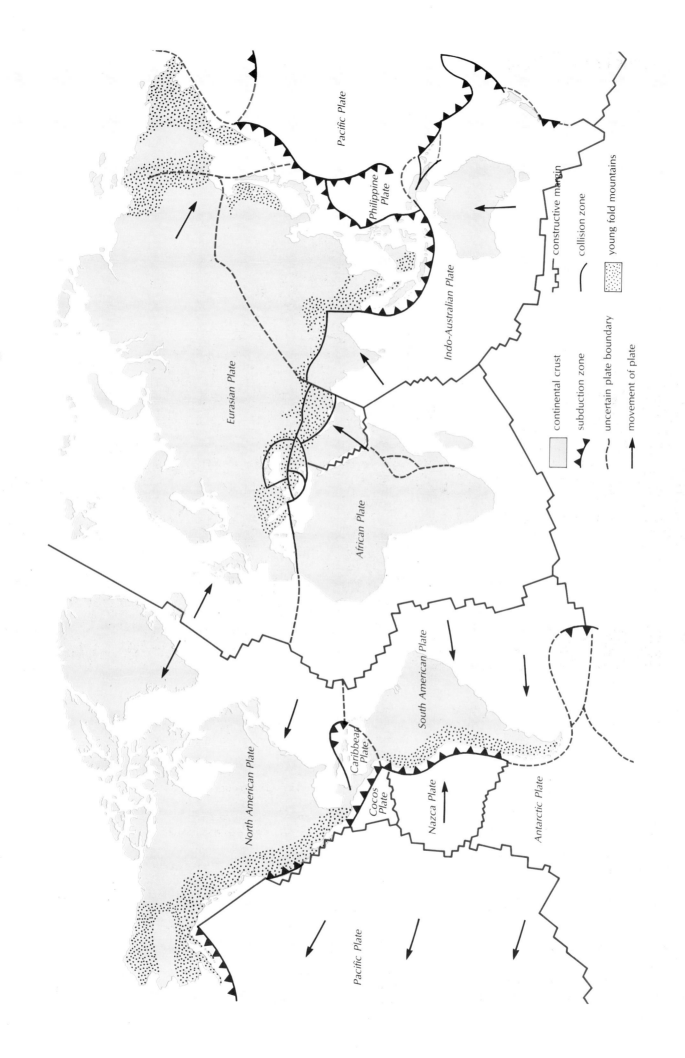

Pacific Plate

Philippine Plate

Indo-Australian Plate

Eurasian Plate

African Plate

North American Plate

Caribbean Plate

Cocos Plate

Nazca Plate

South American Plate

Antarctic Plate

Pacific Plate

constructive margin

collision zone

young fold mountains

continental crust

subduction zone

uncertain plate boundary

movement of plate

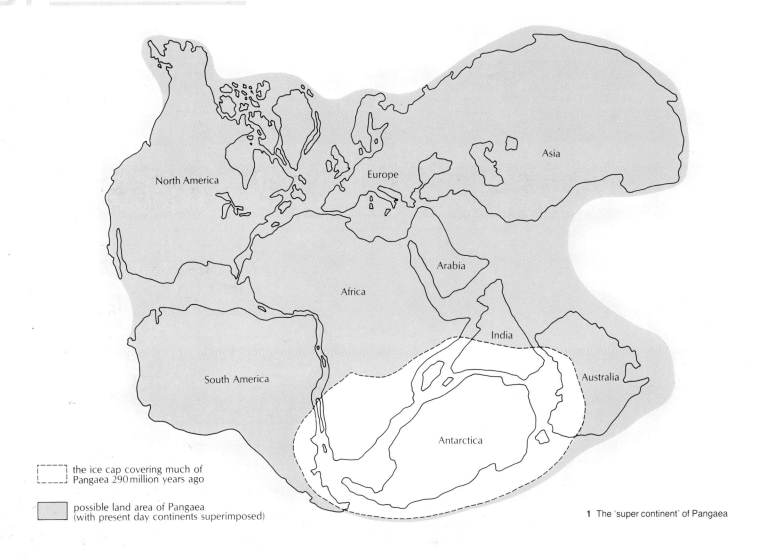

the ice cap covering much of
Pangaea 290 million years ago

possible land area of Pangaea
(with present day continents superimposed)

1 The 'super continent' of Pangaea

In the 1960s a theory was suggested which helps to explain the mysteries listed on page 78. This is the theory of plate tectonics. It says that the thin shell of solid rock forming the Earth's crust and the top of its *mantle* is divided into a number of separate pieces called plates (see Visual 2, page 79). These plates are moving slowly across the surface of the planet. Beneath the plates are the rocks of the mantle. These are so hot and under such pressure that they are liquid, or molten.

In effect, the plates are 'floating' on the molten rocks of the mantle. It is thought that giant *convection currents* occur in the liquid mantle. As these currents circulate, they drag the floating plates with them. The continents and oceans, which lie on top of the plates, are also moved. Where the plates meet, violent changes happen. The margins of the plates seem to be of three kinds: constructive, destructive and conservative.

The movements of the plates in the past provide the answer to several of the Earth's geological mysteries. For example, the ice age which affected the southern continents 290 million years ago, can be easily understood if the continents are fitted together as shown in Visual 1. This 'super continent' has been called Pangaea (from the Greek meaning 'all land'). Pangaea is thought to have started to break apart about 200 million years ago. Since then, the continents have been slowly drifting apart. In fact, this drifting is still going on. Slowly but surely North America, which was once joined on to Europe, is moving further away from Europe. The map of the world with which we are familiar is just a single frame in an immensely long film!

1 *Six problems facing Earth scientists in the 1960s are listed on page 78. Copy out the list and try to explain the possible solution to each problem.*

2 *Write a short article for a Californian newspaper explaining why the state faces the threat of earthquakes. Include a diagram in your article.*

3 *Design and write a short pamphlet for visitors to Iceland explaining why the island has so much volcanic activity.*

4 *'The map of the world with which we are familiar is just a single frame in an immensely long film!' Explain what this statement means.*

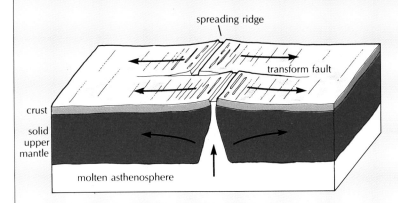

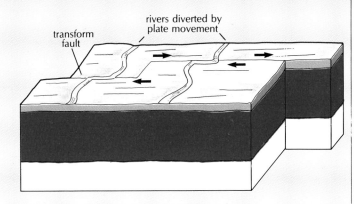

CONSTRUCTIVE PLATE MARGINS occur where new crust is formed. The oceanic ridges are constructive margins. Two plates are moving apart and magma rises to the surface from below. The Mid Atlantic Ridge is an example. This is a range of volcanoes running in a narrow line beneath the middle of the Atlantic Ocean. In places these volcanoes are so high that they reach the ocean surface to form islands, such as Iceland. Constructive margins on land are called rift valleys.

CONSERVATIVE PLATE MARGINS occur where two plates simply move slowly past each other. Such margins are also called transform faults. No crust is created or destroyed at conservative margins and there is no volcanic activity. However, the movement is not continuous but occurs as a series of jerks which cause earthquakes. An example of a conservative plate margin occurs in California where the Pacific plate is moving past the North American plate.

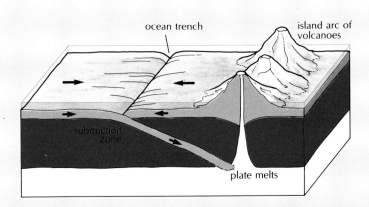

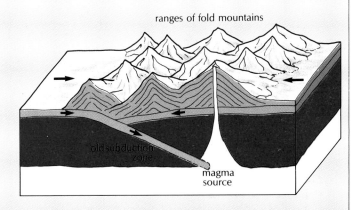

DESTRUCTIVE PLATE MARGINS occur where crust is being destroyed. There are two types of destructive margin: subduction zones and collision zones.

Subduction zones occur at the deep ocean trenches where the sea floor is pulled down as one plate slowly passes under another. The subduction zone is marked by earthquakes. As the oceanic crust plunges into the mantle it melts and rises to the surface where it erupts as lava. When this happens right out in the ocean, a chain of volcanic islands, called an island arc, is formed. An example is the Aleutian trench, where the Pacific plate passes beneath the North American plate. The Aleutian Islands mark the island arc.

Collision zones occur where two plates carrying continental crust collide. The continental crust crumples up to form fold mountains. An example is the Himalayan mountain range, formed where the Indo-Australian plate is colliding with the Eurasian plate.

The Old Man and the Mountain

There ain't nothing that mountain can do to scare me off. My home and my life are here. I'll never leave Spirit Lake.' Harry Truman, 84, refused to obey the order of sheriff's deputies to leave his home. Harry laughed at their appeals: 'There's no danger. I've lived here years. I'll be safe. Leave me alone.'

On four of the ... Lent we shall be co... four churches of t... for a series of 'Le... Methodist Church. 17th, 24th, 31st and

The Speakers invited

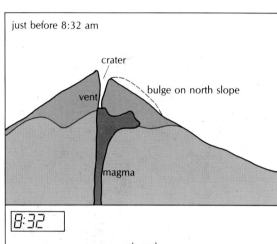

just before 8:32 am

crater
vent
bulge on north slope
magma

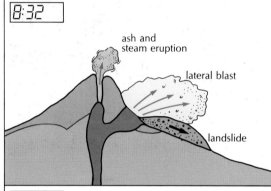

8:32

ash and steam eruption
lateral blast
landslide

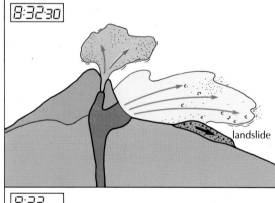

8:32:30

landslide

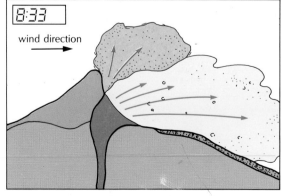

8:33

wind direction

Television crews, newspaper and radio reporters visited the old man's lakeside lodge. Harry Truman was seen on television screens around the world. He became known as 'the man the mountain could not move'.

Harry Truman's brief spell of fame ended at about 8.35 on the morning of 18 May 1980. The volcano Mount St Helens erupted with a force equal to a 10 megatonne nuclear bomb. This was five hundred times the power of the nuclear bomb which destroyed the Japanese city of Hiroshima during World War Two. Harry Truman's lodge was just 8 km from the eruption. A searing blast of hot air, ash and dust engulfed the lodge, burying it under 100 m of debris. Harry Truman had no chance.

Sixty other people died that morning, as Mount St Helens created hell on earth. The eruption happened after six weeks of preliminary activity. The 'countdown to disaster' is shown below. At 8.32 am on 18 May an earthquake caused a landslide, as the bulging section on the northern side of the volcano slumped away. The landslide careered down the valley of the River Toutle at a speed of over 250 km per hour, destroying everything in its path, including Harry Truman.

The landslide exposed the magma inside the volcano. This caused the volcano to explode sideways in a lateral blast of gas and steam which was heard 300 km away. The blast flattened millions of 50 m high coniferous trees over an area of 520 square km.

COUNTDOWN TO DISASTER	
20 March	A minor earthquake measuring 4.1 on the Richter Scale took place under Mount St Helens.
22 March	A stronger earthquake, measuring 4.3 on the Richter Scale.
24 March	A series of earthquakes occurred, the strongest measuring 4.4.
26 March	Earthquakes continued at the rate of six or seven per hour.
27 March	A minor explosive eruption of ash and smoke occurred. Two craters appeared on the volcano's summit. By 4 April the two craters had joined to form a single large crater.
8 April	Minor eruptions had become an almost daily event; on 8 April a stronger eruption occurred. Activity slowed during April, but a growing bulge had appeared on the north side of the volcano.
10 May	The bulge was now 100 m high and growing at 2 m a day. An earthquake measuring 4.9 occurred.
18 May	8.32 am. An earthquake measuring 5.0 occurred. As Visual 1 shows, the earthquake caused a landslide as the bulging section slumped. This exposed lava inside the volcano which erupted explosively.

1 The eruption of Mount St Helens

The blast was followed seconds later by an eruption which threw 400 million tonnes of ash and dust into the atmosphere. Rocks were ejected also. Pumice (spongy lumps of lava) rained down on to the surrounding area. Such rocks are known as volcanic bombs or pyroclasts.

The ash cloud billowed north eastwards, turning day into night and covering a vast area with ash. The ash blocked roads and choked rivers, causing flooding. It damaged crops and killed livestock. The ash cloud, slowly thinning out, crossed the United States in three days and travelled right around the world in just 17 days. A newspaper stated: 'Don't worry if you can't visit Washington State this year, because Washington State is coming to you, courtesy of Mount St Helens!'

The eruption blew away a cubic kilometre of the volcano's summit, reducing its height from 2950 m to 2560 m and leaving a vast crater. There were further eruptions on 25 May and 12 June, with a number of minor eruptions continuing into 1981. Mount St Helens had become known throughout the world and provided a grim reminder of the awesome powers of Nature.

2 The mountain explodes

3 Conifers are laid flat by the blast

1 *Mount St Helens is in Washington State. Find Washington State in your atlas and describe its location within the United States.*

2 *Using the 'countdown to disaster', write about the eruption of Mount St Helens on 18 May 1980. What caused the eruption and what happened afterwards?*

3 *Visual 4 is a map of the Mount St Helens area. Copy the map and draw isolines (contours joining points of equal ash fallout) at intervals of 1 cm.*

4 a) *In which direction did most of the ash travel?*

   b) *How far from the volcano was the furthest point to be covered by: i) 5 cm ii) 3 cm of ash?*

   c) *Calculate the area which was completely devastated by the eruption.*

5 *If the ash cloud crossed the United States in three days, at what speed did it travel in kilometres per hour? (Use your atlas to calculate the width of the United States.)*

6 *Working in pairs:*

   a) *Imagine that one of you is Harry Truman and the other a radio reporter. The reporter is there to do an interview. The date is 17 May 1980. Carry out that interview. Use a cassette recorder if you can.*

   b) *Now change roles. Record an interview between a reporter and a holidaymaker who managed to escape from the eruption.*

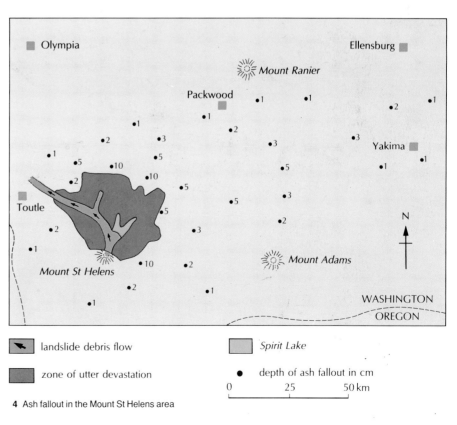

landslide debris flow

zone of utter devastation

Spirit Lake

• depth of ash fallout in cm

0   25   50 km

4 Ash fallout in the Mount St Helens area

VOLCANOES

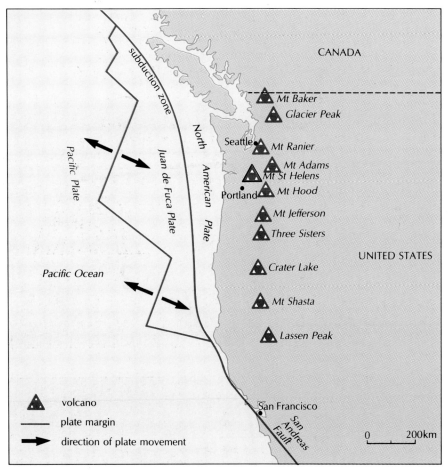

1 The Cascade Range of volcanoes

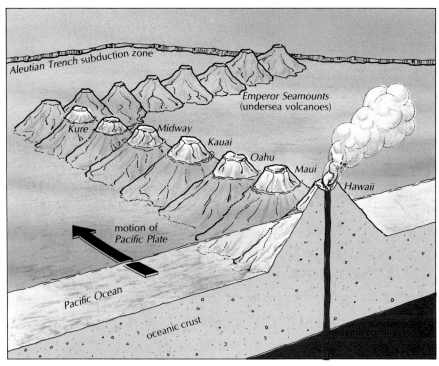

2 The volcanic chain formed by the Hawaiian hot spot

What caused the tremendous eruption of Mount St Helens? The theory of plate tectonics has the likely answer. Off the coast of Washington State is the small Juan de Fuca plate, which lies between the huge Pacific and North American plates. At the boundary between the North American plate and the Juan de Fuca plate is a subduction zone, where one plate is being forced down beneath the other. The Juan de Fuca plate is disappearing at a rate of 3 cm per year under the North American plate.

At a depth of some 100 km beneath Washington State, the Juan de Fuca plate starts to melt. Molten rocks, under great pressure, have punched their way up through the crust to the Earth's surface. This has created the Cascade Range of volcanoes, of which Mount St Helens is just one (Visual 1).

Volcanic activity happens both at the subduction zones and the constructive plate margins. There are a few examples of volcanoes occurring in areas far from plate margins, for example the Hawaiian Islands. Such volcanoes are caused by 'hot spots', which are fixed sources of magma deep beneath the crust. The hot spot continuously blasts lava through the Earth's crust. Since the crust is moving and the hot spot is stationary, the path of the crust can be followed by the trail of volcanoes running away from the hot spot (Visual 2). There are thought to be over 30 hot spots around the world, including those beneath Tahiti, the Azores and Yellowstone (United States).

Volcanoes and People

Volcanoes can be killers. The 61 victims of Mount St Helens are but a small fraction of the 400 000 people estimated to have been killed by volcanoes since the 1500s. It is not simply the direct effects of lava and ash which kill; volcanic eruptions often trigger secondary effects which may be just as deadly. Tidal waves, more correctly called tsunamis, killed over 36 000 people when Krakatoa erupted in 1883. Mudflows, triggered by the eruption of the volcano Nevado del Ruiz, killed 20 000 in Colombia in 1985. The town of Armero was wiped out, engulfed by a broad river of mud. Despite these disasters, volcanoes are less dangerous than earthquakes, mainly because eruptions are usually preceded by clear warning signs such as the emission of steam or ash.

Volcanoes can also be helpful to people. Volcanic soils are rich in the minerals and other nutrients which plants need. These highly fertile soils explain why there are often dense populations in volcanic areas. The chemicals produced by volcanoes, such as sulphur, can be extracted. The pumice and basalt can provide valuable building materials. The heat from the volcanic areas (geothermal heat) can be tapped, as in Iceland, Northern Italy and New Zealand. Volcanoes also attract tourists, which can boost the incomes of the local inhabitants.

1 *Explain the probable cause of the eruption of Mount St Helens, using a diagram to help you.*

2 *Hawaii is nowhere near a plate margin, yet the islands are all volcanoes. How were the Hawaiian islands formed?*

3 *Make a list of the ways in which volcanoes can be useful to people.*

4 *Using the information on these pages, explain what each of the following features are, and how they were formed: fissure eruption caldera sill dyke batholith.*

5 *You are a geologist studying the volcano Sierra Granada in the Andes Mountains of South America. You believe that the volcano is about to erupt.*

   a) *Prepare a press release of not more than 200 words explaining in simple terms why you think the volcano will erupt. You should include a drawing showing the cause of volcanic activity in the Andes (a subduction zone).*

   b) *Prepare a report setting out the possible effects and side effects of a major eruption of the volcano. Include a suggestion for actions to be taken by the authorities before the eruption.*

TYPES OF VOLCANO

Mount St Helens is an example of a composite volcano. This means that it is composed of alternate layers of lava and ash. Most volcanoes are of this type. They have a gently sloping concave shape. Other volcanoes are formed almost entirely of lava. The shape of these volcanoes depends upon the type of lava which erupts. Basic lava flows easily and covers a vast distance. It produces very gently sloping volcanic cones. An example is Mauna Loa in the Hawaiian Islands, which rises 9 km above the sea-bed and has a diameter of over 250 km at its base. Such basic lava cones are also called shield volcanoes. Acid lavas are much thicker (viscous) and do not flow very easily. Acid lava cones are very steep. An example is the Puy de Dome in the Auvergne region of France. This volcano last erupted over a million years ago and is thus called an extinct volcano.

Sometimes the eruption of a volcano can be so explosive that the volcano itself is destroyed. This was the case in 1883 when the volcanic island of Krakatoa in Indonesia blew itself apart. The shattered remains of the volcanic cone is called a caldera. A caldera can also be produced by the rather less dramatic process of collapsing. The caldera of Crater Lake in Oregon was probably produced in this way.

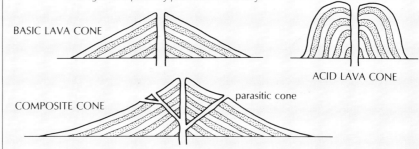

BASIC LAVA CONE

ACID LAVA CONE

COMPOSITE CONE   parasitic cone

OTHER VOLCANIC LANDFORMS

Volcanic landforms can be divided into *extrusive* and *intrusive* forms. The major type of extrusive landform is the volcano, but another important form is the fissure eruption. Lava erupts along a broad crack or fissure and may flow across a vast area. South of Mount St Helens in the United States is the Columbia Plateau, which covers 600 000 square km. This plateau is made of lava, over a kilometre thick in places, and represents a series of outpourings over a long period of time.

Intrusive landforms occur when the lava rising through the Earth's crust does not reach the surface. Magma which solidifies in joints produces a dyke. Magma which solidifies along bedding planes produces a sill. Larger, shapeless masses of molten rock that solidify within the crust are called batholiths. Similar, but smaller, intrusions are called bosses. Sometimes the magma forces the rock strata to fold upwards to create a dome within which a laccolith is formed.

1 A modern block smashed by Mexico's earthquake

At 7.19 am on Thursday, 19 September 1985, the world's largest city was struck by a devastating earthquake. Pavements buckled, the earth cracked open, buildings collapsed and thousands died. Thirty six hours later, at 7.38 pm, Mexico City was shaken by a second earthquake, almost as damaging as the first. Thirty thousand people were killed by the two earthquakes. Over 900 apartment blocks and high-rise buildings collapsed, 500 schools and over half the hospital rooms in the city were wrecked. Electricity and telephone lines were cut. Water and sewage pipes were ripped open, spewing their contents into the shattered streets.

One of the worst scenes of tragedy was the Central Hospital; the 12 storey building was reduced to a pile of rubble only four storeys high. Some 1000 patients and medical staff were killed. Rescue workers swarmed over the rubble, digging, hammering, tearing with their bare hands at the concrete, pulling crushed and broken bodies from the remains of the hospital. Yet amidst this disaster there was a miracle; 58 new-born babies were extracted alive from the wreckage, some several days after the earthquake.

International aid poured into Mexico City. Aircraft flew in doctors, medical supplies, clothing and tents from countries throughout the world. Communist countries, capitalist countries, wealthy and poor all contributed.

The earthquake was caused by movement along the subduction zone off the Mexican coast. Here the Cocos oceanic plate is sliding beneath the North American continental plate. The movement is neither smooth nor regular. Great pressure builds up over a period of many years. This pressure is released in just a few seconds as an earthquake. An earthquake begins at a point within the crust called the focus. The point on the surface, directly above the focus, is called the epicentre. The epicentre of the Mexican earthquake was 50 km off the west coast and 400 km from Mexico City. The city was especially vulnerable to the earthquake because it is built on the soft mud and peat of a drained lake.

Another factor in the damage to Mexico City was the buildings themselves. Mexican engineers have a high reputation for designing buildings to resist earthquakes, but it has been claimed that the building regulations have not always been fully enforced. To make as much money as possible, some builders used cheap materials and took short cuts. Their poor workmanship resulted in unsafe buildings. Most of these were in overcrowded, poor areas of the inner city. In some parts of Mexico City only a few buildings were damaged, almost all of them modern high-rise blocks. The 300-year-old palaces and convents of the central area of Mexico City survived, although they lie in the heart of the worst-hit area where more recent buildings collapsed. The older buildings had survived over a dozen serious earthquakes since they were built; the more modern buildings were unable to survive one earthquake. It seems that greed and corruption caused many unnecessary deaths.

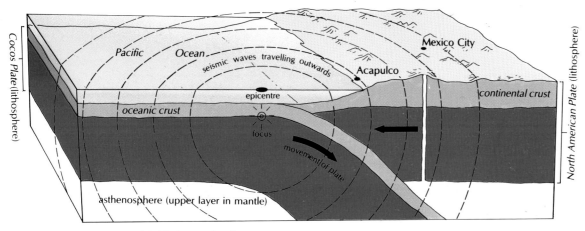

2 The cause of the Mexican earthquakes

Position on Mercalli Scale	Effects	Position on Richter Scale	Position on Mercalli Scale	Effects	Position on Richter Scale
I	Detected only by seismographs	Under 3.5	VII	Panic, walls crack, difficult to stand	5.5 - 6.0
II	Few people notice	3.5	VIII	Chimneys fall, branches break from trees	6.1 - 6.7
III	Hanging objects swing	4.2	IX	Ground cracks, houses collapse, pipes crack	6.8 - 6.9
IV	Windows rattle, felt by people walking	4.4	X	Many houses collapse, landslides occur, ground opens wide	7.0 - 7.3
V	Sleepers awakened, bells toll	4.8	XI	Few buildings survive, bridges collapse	7.4 - 8.1
VI	Felt by all, trees sway, objects fall	4.9 - 5.4	XII	Total destruction	8.1 - 8.9

3 The Mercalli and Richter Scales of earthquake intensity

1 a) When exactly did the two 1985 Mexican earthquakes occur?

   b) Where was the epicentre of the earthquakes?

2 a) How far from the epicentre was Mexico City?

   b) Describe some of the effects of the earthquakes in Mexico City.

3 Using Visual 2 to help you, explain what caused the Mexican earthquakes.

4 Visual 3 shows two scales for measuring how severe an earthquake is. The first 1985 Mexican earthquake registered 7.8 on the Richter Scale.
What would have been the probable effects in Mexico City if this earthquake had measured: a) 4.3 b) 6.9 c) 8.6 on the Richter Scale?

5 The Mexican earthquakes were a natural event; there was nothing people could have done to stop them. In what ways did people contribute to the effects of the earthquakes?

6 On the right is a list of some of the major earthquakes between 1970 and 1985.

   a) On an outline map of the world, mark on the location of the earthquakes.

   b) Add to your map the margins of the Earth's crustal plates (see Visual 2, page 79).

   c) How close is the relationship between the locations of the earthquakes and the margins of the crustal plates?

YEAR	AREA AFFECTED	DEATHS
1970	Peru	20 000
1970	South Turkey	1 800
1971	California, USA	60
1972	Nicaragua	12 000
1975	Eastern Turkey	2 300
1976	Guatemala	23 000
1976	Tangshan, China	450 000
1976	Irian, Indonesia	9 000
1976	North East Italy	925
1976	Mindanao, Philippines	5 000
1976	Eastern Turkey	3 800
1980	Southern Italy	3 000
1982	Marib, North Yemen	2 000
1982	North Afghanistan	515
1983	Japan	110
1985	Mexico City	30 000

An earthquake has occurred in California in the United States. The epicentre is 50 km east of the city of Los Angeles. The shock waves from the earthquake have caused destruction in San Fernando, Pasadena, Long Beach and in the centre of Los Angeles itself. The earthquake happened at 10.15 am and measured 7.7 on the Richter Scale. Early reports indicate great loss of life, damage to buildings and disruption of services.

Your Assignment
You are a journalist working for a London newspaper.

○ Produce a dramatic headline and a story which emphasize the human tragedy of the earthquake.

○ Include an analysis section which explains why the earthquake has happened in this particular location.

Resources

1 The telex from Worldwide Press Agency.

2 Encyclopaedia entry for Los Angeles.

3 The photographs showing destruction.

4 Your atlas.

Work Programme

1 Your report should include a dramatic headline and should be laid out in the style of a newspaper.

2 You should include a main section detailing the human impact of the earthquake and a briefer section explaining why the earthquake happened at that particular location.

3 Your report and analysis should be illustrated with relevant maps and drawings.

87-02-06   12:30

ATTENTION FLEET STREET   FROM: WORLDWIDE PRESS AGENCY

VERY STRONG EARTHQUAKE STRUCK LOS ANGELES AREA 10:15 A.M.
PACIFIC SUMMER TIME STOP 7.7 RICHTER STOP EARLY REPORTS STATE
HEAVY CASUALTIES STOP LOS ANGELES CENTRAL HOSPITAL HAS
BROADCAST EMERGENCY APPEAL FOR BLOOD DONORS STOP SEVERAL
FREEWAY BRIDGES COLLAPSED STOP SHOCK WAVES FELT IN THIS
OFFICE STOP FIRES AND WRECKED BUILDINGS OBSERVED FROM THIS
OFFICE STOP GOVERNOR HAS DECLARED A DISASTER AREA AND
APPEALED TO FEDERAL GOVERNMENT FOR ASSISTANCE STOP

UNITED STATES OF AMERICA

Los Angeles

Los Angeles is a sprawling city with a population of 12 million. It covers over 6 000 square km. Outside the central area the city consists almost entirely of detached houses and bungalows linked by a complex network of roads and freeways. Los Angeles' major industries are aerospace, electronics, motor vehicles and textiles. Los Angeles is in a low rainfall, semi-desert area. Its high water demands are met by transferring water by aqueduct from the River Colorado 400 km to the east and from the Owens Valley 400 km to the north. The San Andreas fault system runs beneath Los Angeles. In this area there are several parallel faults.

UNITED STATES OF AMERICA

San Francisco

FAULTING AND FOLDING

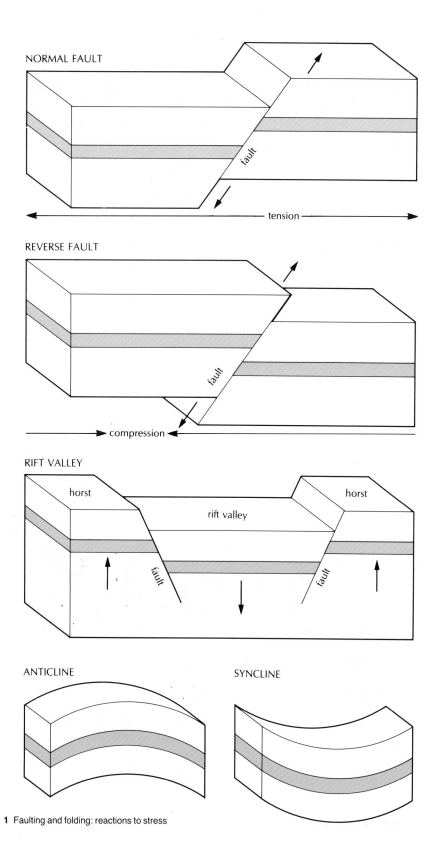

NORMAL FAULT

tension

REVERSE FAULT

fault

compression

RIFT VALLEY

horst

rift valley

horst

fault

fault

ANTICLINE

SYNCLINE

1 Faulting and folding: reactions to stress

Earthquakes. Volcanoes. Plate movements. These create great stresses and strains in the rocks of the Earth's crust. The rocks can react to this stress in two ways. They may crumple through the process of folding or crack through the process of faulting. Visual 1 shows faulting and folding.

Faulting
Visual 1 shows the main landforms created by faulting. The Scottish Lowlands are a rift valley over 80 km wide (Visual 3). The Lowlands sank between two parallel faults, the Highland Boundary Fault to the north and the Southern Upland Fault to the south. The faulting caused volcanic eruptions, which formed lines of hills, such as the Ochil Hills, rising to 600 m above the surrounding plain.

This ancient faulting has had a tremendous effect upon the geography of Scotland, not only in the landscape but also in human activities. Seventy-five per cent of the population of Scotland live in the rift valley. This is the largest area of lowland in the country. The climate is warmer and drier than in the highlands and there are deep soils suitable for farming. The lowland has also made the development of roads and railways easier.

Folding
Folding has important effects on the landscape. Study Visual 2 which shows the London Basin. This is a syncline formed by a ripple from the great collision between the African and Eurasian plates which created the Alps. The syncline has been eroded and recent deposition has filled in the centre, but the landscape of the area cannot be understood without realizing the importance of the folding. This folding affects today's landscape and also London's water supply. Rain which falls on to the Chiltern Hills and North Downs drains through the permeable chalk until it reaches the water table. The water table is higher under the hills surrounding London than in the London Basin itself. This means that the water below London is under pressure. Wells sunk down to the chalk aquifer release the pressure and the water rushes up to the surface. This type of well is called an artesian well and the syncline itself is an example of an artesian basin. London obtains about one-tenth of its water from wells. The water now has to be pumped to the surface because of over-use and there are fears that the wells, used for centuries, may soon run dry.

To the south of the London Basin lie the North Downs, the Weald and the South Downs (Visual 2). The rocks of this region were upfolded into a large anticline by the Alpine folding. The folding weakened the top of the anticline by stretching and cracking the rocks. Erosion has removed the younger rocks. Only the sides, or limbs, of the anticline remain. The scarp slopes of the North and South Downs are separated by a distance of over 40 km, where the chalk has been eroded away. Some of the older rocks exposed by the erosion are hard and some are soft. The harder sandstones form escarpments and the softer clays form vales. Escarpments and vales are often found in pairs. The folding has also affected the coastal scenery. Cliffs are formed where the chalk and sandstone reach the coast. Examples are the chalk cliffs of Dover and Beachy Head and the sandstone cliffs of Hastings. Where the softer clays reach the coast, there are bays and marshes such as Romney Marsh and the Pevensey Levels.

1 *Draw your own diagrams to explain the formation of:*
   a) anticlines and synclines   b) rift valleys.
2 *How has folding affected London's water supply?*
3 *Why was the top of the Wealden Anticline easily eroded?*
4 *Study Visual 3.*
   a) Explain how the rift valley was formed.
   b) How does the rift valley affect: i) the landscape
       ii) the human activities of central Scotland?

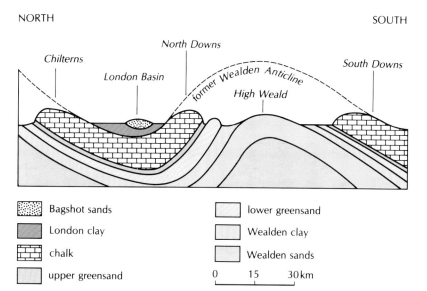

Bagshot sands

London clay

chalk

upper greensand

lower greensand

Wealden clay

Wealden sands

0   15   30 km

2 A section through the London Basin and the Weald

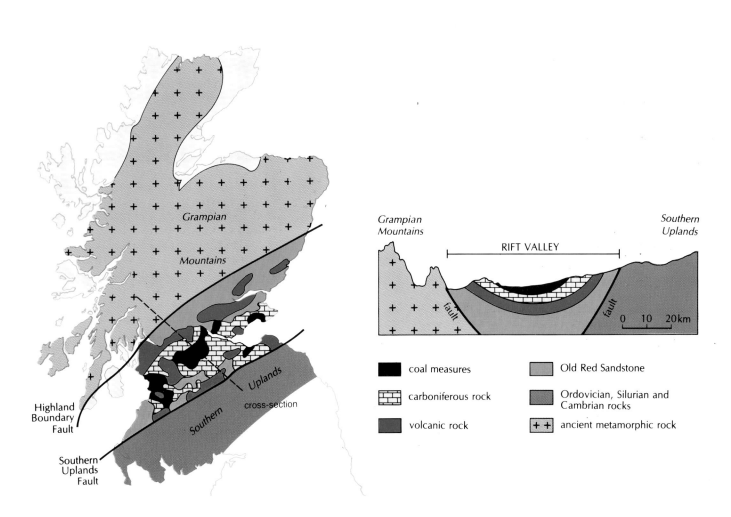

coal measures

carboniferous rock

volcanic rock

Old Red Sandstone

Ordovician, Silurian and Cambrian rocks

ancient metamorphic rock

3 The Scottish Rift Valley

ASSIGNMENT NINE
The Quality of the Environment

A

B

C

D

Throughout this book we have been concerned with the interaction of people and the natural landscape. Geographers are increasingly interested in the quality of the environment, both in rural and urban areas.

Your Assignment
- Consider some examples of different landscapes.
- Carry out your own fieldwork.

Resources
1 The photographs A–H showing town and country scenes.
2 Visual 1.

Work Programme A

Study the four scenes shown above. They are all taken in the same city.

1 Which area would you prefer to live in? Give reasons.

2 Which area would you prefer to visit? Give reasons.

3 Rank the scenes in order of their attractiveness to you.

4 Rank the scenes in order of their value to society.

5 Compare your answers with those of your neighbour.

Your answers will probably differ. There are, of course, no correct answers. Each person will have his or her own ideas as to what is attractive, since 'beauty is in the eye of the beholder'!

Work Programme B

Now study the four scenes on the opposite page.

1 Answer the five questions listed in Work Programme A.

2 Did you find this easier or harder than before? Why?

3 It is possible to adopt a more scientific approach when evaluating a landscape. One way is to consider a number of words which might describe a place. Then allocate a points score (Visual 1). If, for example, you found a place very attractive, you might give it five points; if it were ugly you might give it only one point. Below is a list of 10 word pairs:

HIGH QUALITY	5	4	3	2	1	LOW QUALITY
attractive						ugly
peaceful						noisy
interesting						boring
stimulating						depressing
unpolluted						polluted
special						ordinary
tidy						untidy
safe						dangerous
uncongested						congested
like						dislike

TOTAL POINTS: . . . . . . out of 50

4 Copy the list. Add five more suitable word pairs to it.

5 Apply the list to the photographs.

6 Compare your results with your neighbour's, and discuss any differences.

E

F

G

H

8ᵀᴴ MARCH.

St AUGUSTINES AVENUE.

HIGH QUALITY.	5	4	3	2	1	LOW QUALITY.
		✓				Ugly
Attractive		✓				Noisy
Peaceful			✓			Boring
Interesting			✓			Dirty
Clean		✓				Untidy
Tidy			✓			Depressing
Stimulating		✓				Dangerous
Safe			✓			Impersonal
Welcoming						Badly designed
Well designed						Dislike
Like						
TOTAL			out of 50.			

1 Using a points score to evaluate a landscape

Work Programme C

It is easy to apply variations of the above method to actual places. For example, you could make a survey of a shopping centre (Visual 1) to include the following words:

HIGH QUALITY	5	4	3	2	1	LOW QUALITY
attractive						ugly
tidy						untidy
clean						dirty
wide pavements						narrow pavements
busy						deserted
uncongested						congested
welcoming						impersonal
well designed						badly designed
simple layout						complex layout
like						dislike

TOTAL POINTS: . . . . out of 50

Similar surveys could be made of streets, housing estates, industrial estates, parks and so on.

1 Working in a small group, decide on an area which you can easily visit to conduct a landscape evaluation.

2 Decide the purpose of your survey.

3 Design a survey list to measure the quality of the area.

4 Visit the area and carry out your survey.

5 Write up your results and compare them with other groups.

6 If several areas of a town or village have been surveyed, you could make a map showing the variations of landscape or environmental quality. (This assumes that the purpose of the survey is the same for each area.)

GLOSSARY

Acid rain   Rainwater or snow which has become slightly acidic through dissolving sulphur dioxide gas held in the atmosphere. Sulphur dioxide is discharged into the atmosphere mainly by the chimneys of power stations and factories which burn oil or coal as their fuel. Winds in the upper atmosphere may carry the droplets of weak sulphuric acid hundreds of kilometres from where they were formed, before they fall on land or water.

Alluvium   Earth, sand, gravel and other fine-grained materials deposited by rivers or floods.

Asthenosphere   The layer of the Earth immediately below the plates (lithosphere) and on which they move.

Catchment   The area from which a stream receives its water. It is also called a drainage basin.

Convection current   The current produced when the bottom part of a volume of fluid is heated. The hotter bottom part, being of lower density, rises above the colder part, which moves down to take its place. This sets up a circulation of fluid in which heat is carried from the hotter to the colder part.

Core   The central spherical part of the Earth, probably about 7000 km in diameter. It comprises an inner solid mass and an outer molten layer. It is believed that the core consists largely of iron.

Crust   The thin, solid, outermost layer of the Earth. It exists in two forms: the continental crust and the thinner oceanic crust which is the floor of the ocean basins. The thickness of the continental crust averages about 40 km, that of the oceanic crust 10 km.

Delta   An area of flat, marshy land, more or less shaped like a triangle, which is found at the mouth of certain rivers. The main river is split into a number of smaller river channels or distributaries. The delta is formed from the alluvium deposited by the river as it slows down on entering the sea or the lake into which it discharges.

Distributary   Any river channel branching out from the main river in a delta.

Ecology   The study of animals and plants in relation to their surroundings and the balance of these relationships. A community of living things and their environment is called an ecosystem. An ecosystem may be as large as an arctic tundra or as small as a pond.

Estuary   The tidal mouth of a river where it enters the sea.

Extrusive vulcanicity   The eruption of molten igneous rock (magma) on to the Earth's surface and the features so produced.

Fault   A crack or fracture in a mass of rock along which there has been a movement (displacement) of rock on one side relative to the other. The displacement may be in any direction.

Flood plain   The flat land forming the floor of a river valley. The area is regularly flooded by the river and is usually composed of sediment deposited by the river.

Fold mountains   Mountains formed by earth movements (folding) which crumpled up the layers of rock.

Freeze–thaw   The alternate freezing and thawing of water trapped within a fissure or crack in a mass of rock. When water freezes, it expands and tends to enlarge any crack it is in. The enlarged crack can then hold more water than before, which will further enlarge the crack on renewed freezing. This action weakens the rock and eventually particles break away from the main body of rock.

Gorge   A deep, narrow section of a river valley with steep sides.

Groyne   A barrier built on a beach to prevent the removal of the beach materials by longshore drift. It extends seawards perpendicular to the coastline. Groynes are usually built in groups, their length, height and distance apart depending on local conditions.

Gully   A narrow channel worn into a soil or rock slope by flowing water.

Horst   An uplifted block of rocks between faults. It is also called a block mountain.

Humidity   The amount of water vapour in the air. On a very humid or 'sticky' day, the air may be almost saturated with water vapour.

Intrusive vulcanicity   The injection of magma into the Earth's crust, where it cools and solidifies beneath the surface.

Isobar   A line drawn on a map through places which have equal atmospheric pressure.

Isohyet   A line drawn on a map through places which have equal amounts of rainfall.

Isohel   A line drawn on a map through place which have equal amounts of sunshine.

Joint   A crack or fracture in a mass of rock along which there has been no movement (displacement) of rock.

Lithosphere   Another name for the plates of the Earth. It consists of the crust and the rigid part of the mantle which lies above the asthenosphere.

Lysimeter   A large, cylindrical, test-piece of soil which is kept in its original position but isolated from the surrounding soil by an open-top container such as an oil drum. It is used to collect and measure drainage water, from which certain soil properties, such as nitrogen loss, can be found.

Magma   Hot, molten rock lying under great pressure below the Earth's solid crust. It originates in the mantle or the melted rocks of the crust. Magma becomes lava when it erupts through a volcanic fissure.

Mantle   The part of the Earth between its solid crust and the core. It is about 2900 km thick and rich in silica.

Mineral   Any naturally occurring substance which has a definite chemical composition. It is often in a crystalline form. Minerals are the building blocks of rocks.

Model   A representation of a real situation in the form of a diagram, mathematical equations or a built-to-scale 'model'.

Multipurpose project   An engineering scheme which has several aims.

Pavement   A flattish area of carboniferous limestone divided into numerous small blocks by deep, wide fissures. From a distance, a limestone pavement (also called a platform) resembles a vast stretch of crazy paving.

Permafrost   Permanently frozen rock or subsoil.

Promontory   A wide structure built pointing towards the sea to reduce the effect of waves on a beach. A promontory is also a point of land which juts out into the sea or a lake.

Salt marsh   An area of flat, marshy ground, on the landward side of a spit or bar, which has salt-loving plants growing on it and is periodically flooded by seawater.

Seismic wave   A shock or quake travelling outwards in all directions from the source of an earthquake. It is also the term used for the shock wave produced by any explosion within the Earth or at its surface.

Spit   A long, narrow section of land built out into the sea by the action of longshore drift. Usually composed of a mixture of sand and shingle.

Storm surge   The build-up of water in narrow sea areas by storm-force winds. A storm surge usually causes serious coastal flooding.

Structure of rock   The number and size of the individual particles of a rock, the joints, bedding planes, folds and faults of the rock.

Tornado   An advancing whirlwind of strongly rising air currents which can tear up trees and buildings in its path.

Vining machine   A self-propelled machine, steered by a driver, which automatically picks such farm produce as peas. It is also called a viner.

Water balance equation   An equation expressing the amount of water flowing in a river at a given time in terms of water inputs and losses.

Water table   The level or surface below which all the pores and fissures in the ground are saturated with water. Where the water table rises above ground level, areas of standing water exist.

Weir   A low dam built across a river to raise its level and control its flow, particularly in dry weather.

INDEX